$1

I Want to See

JESUS

in a NEW

LIGHT

D0012826

Also by Ron Roth, Ph.D.

Books

The Healing Path of Prayer
(with Peter Occhiogrosso)

Holy Spirit

Prayer and the Five Stages of Healing
(with Peter Occhiogrosso)

Audios

The Dark Night of the Soul

Healing Prayers

Holy Spirit

Prayer and the Five Stages of Healing
(two-tape set and six-tape set)

(All of the above titles are available at your local
bookstore, or may be ordered by calling Hay House at
760-431-7695 or 800-654-5126.)

Please visit the Hay House Website at:
www.hayhouse.com
and Ron Roth's Website at: **www.ronroth.com**

I Want to See

JESUS

in a NEW

LIGHT

Healing Reflections for People of all Faiths

Ron Roth, Ph.D.

HAY HOUSE

Hay House, Inc.
Carlsbad, California • Sydney, Australia

Copyright © 2000 by Ron Roth

Published and distributed in the United States by:
Hay House, Inc., P.O. Box 5100, Carlsbad, CA 92018-5100
(800) 654-5126 • (800) 650-5115 (fax)

Editorial: Peter Occhiogrosso, Jill Kramer • *Design:* Summer McStravick

All rights reserved. No part of this book may be reproduced by
any mechanical, photographic, or electronic process, or in the form of
a phonographic recording; nor may it be stored in a retrieval system,
transmitted, or otherwise be copied for public or private use—other than
for "fair use" as brief quotations embodied in articles and reviews without prior written permission of the publisher.

"At the Foot of the Cross," by Ernest Borgnine. Reprinted with
permission from *Guideposts* magazine. Copyright © 1989 by Guideposts,
Carmel, New York 10512.

Cataloging-in-Publication Data is available from the Library of
Congress.

ISBN 1-56170-677-9

03 02 01 00   4 3 2 1
1st printing, April 2000

Printed in the United States of America

I dedicate this book
to all seekers of truth,
regardless of their religious
beliefs and traditions

~ Contents ~

Preface

The name and identity of Jesus Christ has been tied up with the Christian religion for so long that it is difficult for many people to see Jesus as the sacred individual he was, rather than as the founder of a particular church. And yet I have believed for quite some time that the message of Jesus of Nazareth is too valuable to humanity to be confined to only those dogmatic interpretations espoused by the various expressions of institutional Christianity, whether the Roman Catholic or Eastern Orthodox churches, mainline Protestant denominations, or born-again Christian groups. My vision of Jesus transcends all those labels and classifications, with their beliefs and dogma and rules that one must follow.

My personal understanding of Jesus probably fits more closely with the conception of divine masters found in certain Eastern traditions. The founder of the Baha'i Faith, Baha'u'llah, taught that God intervenes in human history through great spiritual messengers such as Abraham, Moses, Krishna, Zoroaster, Buddha, Jesus, and Muhammad, all of whom he called "Manifestations of God." The spiritual traditions they founded, Baha'u'llah declared, "have proceeded from one Source and are the rays of one Light. That they differ from one another is to be attributed to the varying requirements of the ages in which they were promulgated." And in the Hindu holy book known as the *Bhagavad Gita*, the god-man Krishna explains his role as an avatar or incarnation of Vishnu in similar terms:

> *When goodness grows weak,*
> *When evil increases,*
> *I make myself a body.*
> *In every age I come back*
> *To deliver the holy,*
> *To destroy the sin of the sinner,*
> *To establish righteousness.*

Without assailing the claims of those Christians who believe Jesus to be the only begotten Son of God, I prefer to see Jesus in a more universal context. The name *Christ* is simply a translation into Greek of the Hebrew word for *messiah*, which means "anointed." Yet many biblical figures were anointed, including priests and prophets. Indeed, we are all called to be anointed, which is another way of saying "filled with the Spirit."

I do not place Jesus above Krishna, Moses, Lao-tzu, the Buddha, Muhammad, Mary, or any other manifestation of divine wisdom. But since I have studied the life and teachings of Jesus as they appear in the four canonical Gospels and many of the Gnostic Gospels more than I have the teachings of any other divine messenger, I feel most comfortable using his words as a guide to healing. While wrestling with the dogmatizing of his teachings by the Christian churches, I discovered new ways to convey his message to others without the institutional trappings that I believe to be largely irrelevant to his Truth. Jesus came to show us our own divinity, expressed as our ability to heal ourselves and others through love and forgiveness. Anything else is either an elaboration of that Truth or a distraction from it.

You do not need to be Christian or ever to have studied or practiced Christianity to make use of this book. My deepest wish is that these simple meditations will provide a doorway for people of all religious backgrounds to discover Jesus as a great spiritual healer irrespective of any set of dogmatic beliefs. At the same time, I hope that this book will also help those raised in the Christian tradition to see Jesus in an entirely new light, freed of the dogmatic overlays and misinterpretations of the past.

~ *Introduction* ~

How to Use These Healing Meditations

One night many years ago when I was struggling with my spiritual journey—still a Catholic priest but not at all certain I would remain one—I realized that I had grown weary of the dryness of conventional prayer. Following that approach, I usually did all the talking but felt little sense of genuine communion. There must be a better way, I thought, and then I just let go and sat still. Soon I felt a stirring within me, as if someone or something were trying to get my attention. Although I did not recognize it then, I now realize that it was the voice of God who dwells within us all. I did not "hear" a voice somewhere actually speaking, but I distinctly sensed a directive to take up paper and pen and be prepared to write down whatever came to me.

As I did, I was filled with a peace and serenity that at times was so profound that I broke down and sobbed. I began to see visions of Jesus teaching, healing, and speaking to various individuals in the course of his ministry. As the mental visions continued, I began to imagine the responses of those around Jesus at the time. In a sense, I began to get "inside" these people, some of whom are mentioned in the Gospels, some not, and to feel what might have been going through their minds and hearts as they encountered the powerful spiritual forces emanating from the man called Jesus of Nazareth.

Over time, these visions and the accompanying imagined monologues turned into written meditations on Jesus as seen through the eyes of his contemporaries—from his disciples Peter, John, Thomas, and Mary Magdalene to figures whose lives he touched, such as the Canaanite woman and the man healed at the pool of Bethesda.

Some of the characters whose personalities I invoked do not appear in the Gospels at all, but are ordinary people of the sort who might have made up the population of Judea at that time—a cross maker, a merchant, a Jewish nobleman, a Roman silversmith, a paralytic, an innkeeper, a shepherd, and so on. I even included meditations on several people who had powerfully negative responses to Jesus, such as Pontius Pilate, Annas, and Caiphas, and certain Roman and Jewish contemporaries who were puzzled or even infuriated by his message of love and forgiveness.

I often wrote from nine at night until three in the morning, imagining how people I had never met would talk about Jesus. What bound all the characters whose thoughts flowed through my mind was the sense that Jesus had healed not only the blind and the deaf, the lame and the leprous, but that in some fashion he had healed just about everyone with whom he spoke or interacted. During these meditations, I became aware of my own desire for inner healing into wholeness. I realized my need to change my belief system from negative to positive; to be free; to celebrate life; and above all, to heal the doubt, fear, and anxiety that were plaguing me. By allowing myself to experience the fears and anxieties, and the conflicted feelings of self-incrimination and regret that these characters may have felt, I was able to bring my own negative feelings into the light and begin healing them. Moreover, these acts of what I would call "creative spiritual imagination" started me believing that I could influence others through my writing. I didn't levitate, bilocate, or literally see visions and hear voices, but I did open myself up to the possibility of letting God's healing love flow within me.

I did nothing with these writings for 15 years, but in 1986 I decided to compile the meditations into a slim, self-published volume of just a few hundred copies, upon which this book is based, and which ultimately led to my writing two full-length books on prayer and healing. My original idea for the historical figures such as the apostle Peter, John the Baptist, and Mary Magdalene was to take them off the pedestal and place them at floor level, so that when ordinary people read the meditations they might more easily see themselves reflected in these characters. The moment we put the title "Saint" in front of people's names, we elevate them to a level above ourselves, a level to which we can no longer relate. That can be fine if we're striving to emulate their prayer life, but it can impede our ability to identify with them as human beings. The truth is that all the characters Jesus encountered in the Gospels were flawed in some way, yet he accepted them and forgave them their faults. I wanted my readers to see that the same acceptance and forgiveness that Jesus showered on those flawed characters—both the biblical and fictional ones—was available to them.

In my books *The Healing Path of Prayer* and *Prayer and the Five Stages of Healing,* I've tried to make the point that the most important stage of healing we reach is the awareness that we are one with God and are loved by God. That awareness lifts our self-esteem and empowers us to do great things. It may sound simple, and yet my experience is that most people do not feel deeply that they are loved by God. The purpose of the meditations in this book is to facilitate that awareness by allowing the reader to identify with the doubt, fear, guilt, and shame that certain biblical characters experienced. We forget, for instance, that when things got dicey, Peter, the leader of the disciples and the purported founder of the Christian church, denied that he ever knew Jesus! We forget that Thomas had no faith in Christ's ability to transcend death, or that Mary Magdalene, a woman with a past that included demonic possession, was one of the most prominent figures of the early church until her historical role was buried along with the Gnostic Gospels. Instead, we give them all the Hollywood treatment by polishing their images and making them larger than life.

I used the metaphor of Hollywood image-makers for a reason. Some years after my self-published book came out, I happened to read a story by actor Ernest Borgnine that bore a fascinating parallel to my own experience with these meditations. Borgnine, who won an Oscar for his role in *Marty* in 1955, felt that the movie role that most changed his life was not in *that* film but in the wonderful 1976 film *Jesus of Nazareth*, directed by Franco Zeffirelli, an eight-hour miniseries that is still shown on television every year around Easter time. Jesus was played by the fine British actor Robert Powell; Olivia Hussey portrayed Mary, his mother; Anne Bancroft was Mary Magdalene; and Borgnine had a small but crucial role as the centurion whose servant Jesus healed and who was later present at the crucifixion. As Borgnine tells it:

> When it came time for my scene during the crucifixion, the weather was chill and gray. The camera was to be focused on me at the foot of the cross, and so it was not necessary for Robert Powell, the actor who portrayed Jesus, to be there. Instead, Zeffirelli put a chalk mark on a piece of scenery beside the cameraman. "I want you to look up at that mark," he told me, "as if you were looking at Jesus."
>
> I hesitated. Somehow I wasn't ready. I was uneasy.

"Do you think it would be possible for some-body to read from the Bible the words Jesus said as He hung on the cross?" I asked.

I knew the words well from the days of my childhood in an Italian-American family in Connecticut, and I'd read them in preparation for the film. Even so, I wanted to hear them now.

"I will do it myself," Zeffirelli said. He found a Bible, opened it to the Book of Luke, and signaled for the camera to start rolling.

As Zeffirelli began reading Christ's words aloud, I stared up at that chalk mark, thinking what might have gone through the centurion's mind.

That poor Man up there, I thought. *I met Him when He healed my servant who is like a son to me. Jesus says He is the Son of God, an unfortunate claim during these perilous times. But I know he is innocent of any crime.*

"Father, forgive them; for they know not what they do." The voice was Zeffirelli's, but the words burned into me—the words of Jesus (Luke 23:34-46).

Forgive me, Father, for even being here, was the cen-turion's prayer that formed in my thoughts. *I am so ashamed, so ashamed.*

"Verily I say unto thee, today shalt thou be with me in paradise," said Jesus to the thief hanging next to Him.

If Jesus can forgive that criminal, then He will for-give me, I thought. *I will lay down my sword and retire to my little farm outside of Rome.*

Then it happened.

As I stared upward, instead of the chalk mark, I suddenly saw the face of Jesus Christ, lifelike and clear. It was not the face of Robert Powell I was used to seeing, but the most beautiful, gentle visage I have ever known. Pain-seared, sweat-stained, with blood flowing down from thorns pressed deep, His face was still filled with compassion. He looked down at me through tragic, sorrowful eyes with an expression of love beyond description.

Then His cry rose against the desert wind. Not the voice of Zeffirelli, reading from the Bible, but the voice of Jesus Himself: "Father, into thy hands I commend my spirit."

In awe I watched Jesus' head slump to one side. I knew He was dead. A terrible grief welled within me, and completely oblivious of the camera, I started sobbing uncontrollably.

"Cut!" yelled Zeffirelli. Olivia Hussey and Anne Bancroft were crying, too. l wiped my eyes and looked up again to where I had seen Jesus— He was gone.

Whether I saw a vision of Jesus that windswept day or whether it was only something in my mind, I do not know. It doesn't matter. For I do know that it was a profound spiritual experience and that I have not been quite the same person since. I believe that I take my faith more seriously. I like to think that I'm more forgiving than I used to be. As that centurion learned two thousand years ago, I too have found that you simply cannot come close to Jesus without being changed.*

As I was revising my original book for publication, a program appeared on the ABC news show *20/20* discussing a pioneering treatment for panic disorders and other phobias that in many cases is quick and effective, and may prove to be an alternative to drugs and traditional psychotherapy. Called "intensive exposure therapy," this new treatment invites patients to confront the very things they fear most, and in many cases helps them recover within days. The program showed a young woman with a fear of elevators learning to confront her fear by slowly and repeatedly walking into an elevator, learning to close the door, and eventually, with the help of a trained therapist, riding the elevator. By the end of several hours of treatment, she was able to enter and ride elevators by herself with none of the previous trauma.

---

* Corrie Ten Boom, Elizabeth Sherrill, et al., *Snowflakes in September: Stories about God's Mysterious Ways.* Nashville, Tenn.: Dimensions for Living, 1992.

I believe in the principle behind that approach to healing our fears and anxieties, and I also believe that this book can be therapeutic for you in similar, if less dramatic, ways. The psychologist Carl Jung referred to the often repressed or "dark aspects of the personality" as the *shadow*. "The shadow is a moral problem that challenges the whole ego-personality," Jung wrote, "for no one can become conscious of the shadow without considerable moral effort. To become conscious of it involves recognizing the dark aspects of the personality as present and real. This act is the essential condition for any kind of self-knowledge; therefore, as a rule, it meets with considerable resistance."

Jung nonetheless recommended becoming familiar with the shadow in ourselves and learning to embrace it as a way to heal those dark aspects. We might relate these dark emotions to the concept of negative elementals taught by the Greek mystic Spyros Sathi, known as Daskalos, which I discussed at length in *Prayer and the Five Stages of Healing*. According to Daskalos, elementals take on a life of their own independent of the person who originally projected them, like those thought-forms that are said to be visible to psychics and clairvoyants. We can produce thought-forms and elementals subconsciously or consciously, and though we project them outward, they eventually return to our own subconscious. If we direct negative thoughts of hatred, anger, jealousy, or fear toward someone else who is not receptive to them, those elementals may bounce off them and return to us with increased force. The more we create and project these negative elementals, the more sustenance they take from our unconscious, until they possess us. They are a little like the static electricity that builds up around us from continually rubbing our hand across a carpet. But because we don't like to look at our negative emotional tendencies, we often repeat them until they build up a charge that can genuinely harm us.

The meditations in this book offer a way of defusing or dissipating the negative energies that you may have built up around yourself. At first you may resist seeing these negative elementals as "present and real," as Jung suggested, but if you let yourself be aware of the feelings that arise in you as you read each meditation, you will be bringing them out into the light. It may help if you think of yourself as an actor getting into character, allowing yourself to feel and think what the person in the meditation is feeling and thinking, much the way Ernest Borgnine got into his role as the centurion. It's not a question of losing yourself in a false identity, but of discovering the truth about your own darkest fears and animosities. So even when the character is largely negative, like Herod or the fictitious religion teacher Foronias, let yourself experience his anger or hypocrisy even if it makes you uncomfortable. Think of that woman on the television program with her fear of elevators, acknowledging her fear and stepping into the elevator anyway.

As you immerse yourself in the different personalities presented to me by the Holy Spirit in these meditations by entering into the mind-set of the characters, you will let the therapy of the Holy Spirit work upon your life. Keep in mind that our word *therapy* comes from the Greek *therapeia* and *therapeuein*, which mean "to cure." In that sense, as it says in *A Course in Miracles*, the Holy Spirit is the only therapist. When we meet someone who pushes our buttons and elicits a reaction of anger, fear, or jealousy, we may be receiving a signal from deep within us that something needs to be healed. We may think someone is too cocky, too flashy, too passive, too rich or too poor, and off we go, running the person down with our inner monologue, but all the while it is our own cockiness, or lack of self-confidence, or passivity that needs to be healed. Once we can recognize and confront our particular weakness, however, healing often happens quickly.

To take one example, Romulus is a fictitious Roman soldier who expresses the painfully twisted situation we get into when we do what we are told, even though our gut tells us it's the wrong thing to do. We have all watched films of the Nuremberg Trials and wondered how those evil men could say they were "just following orders" when they set out to exterminate an entire race of people. Hitler's soldiers must have known in their hearts that what they were doing was wrong, we think. Yet how often do we go against our own instincts and do things that are defensible on the surface but that end up hurting other people in even small ways? We just can't help telling a friend some bit of gossip about her partner that may or may not be true but that we sense will hurt her. We tell ourselves that we're just doing her a favor, but that still, small voice inside is telling us that we know better. How do we act? That's what the meditation on Romulus is all about: He did what he was supposed to do, but knows in his gut it was probably not the right thing, and he is suffering for it.

Some of the other meditations in the section titled "Healing the Shadow" present biblical figures such as Pontius Pilate, the high priests Annas and Caiphas, Herod, and fictional creations such as Demetrius the silversmith and Rexus the merchant. As you reflect on these messages and allow your negative feelings to come into the light, you may also become aware of peace and love and the presence of God's Holy Spirit. Don't struggle, but simply rest in His presence and allow Jesus to bring you healing. When I am asked to define *healing*, I describe it as experiencing the peace and love of God in all areas of our lives. These meditations have brought healing to particular areas of my own life over the years. I'm not whole yet, but as I submit more and more to the Voice of God within me, the Holy Spirit who loves, guides, leads, and protects me, I feel myself moving closer to wholeness and holiness. I believe that many of the reflections in this book contain the perceptions we all carry of fear, insecurity, loneliness, and anger—perceptions that are cloudy at best. But allowing the Holy Spirit to speak to us, to bring us God's love and peace, removes the blocks from our perception so that we begin to see Jesus clearly and discover true life and light.

Just as some of the meditations in this book invite you to examine your shadow, others encourage you to experience certain aspects of your personality with which you may not be fully in touch. We all have masculine and feminine aspects blended in our personality, for instance, although we may not value highly enough those aspects that relate to the opposite sex. In our society, men are not often encouraged to develop the feminine traits of being tender and nurturing, nor are women rewarded for bringing out the masculine side of their personalities that might include competitive or assertive tendencies. That fear or lack of acceptance of the opposite gender within us is another area that calls out for healing. I would encourage my male readers not to skip over the meditations on, say, Mary Magdalene or the Samaritan woman, and I would say the same to my female readers regarding the characters of Peter, John, and Pontius Pilate. And nobody needs to feel awkward meditating on the many small children who encountered Jesus.

Although I have been emphasizing the darker aspects of the personalities in these meditations, I don't want to lose sight of the positive message implicit in many of them. Take the example of the Samaritan woman. She had been married a number of times and was living with still another man to whom she was not married, and yet at no time did Jesus attack her or tell her to leave the man she was living with. Jesus saw only her need for love, which he tried to fill by accepting her. The result was that this woman felt so loved by Jesus that she went back and told her whole community about him, and they all came out to see this wondrous person. When I look at the Samaritan woman now, I see my own need for self-acceptance, for forgiving myself for my past faults. We all need to have these kinds of experiences that can heal us on all levels, including the physical, so that we can get on with life and find fulfillment and joy.

A Word about Technique

Although I've referred to this book as a series of meditations, they are not meditations in the conventional sense of closing your eyes and allowing your mind to go blank, chanting a mantra, or following your breath. Rather, they combine silent meditation with more mentally active elements of visualization and contemplation derived from the mystical Christian tradition. In his *Spiritual Exercises,* for instance, the great mystic Ignatius Loyola used a variety of visual techniques to focus on the subject of the meditations he was prescribing, an activity he called "mental representation of place." In one exercise, he writes:

> I will see, in imagination, the great extent and space of the world, where dwell so many different nations and peoples. I will then see particularly the city of Nazareth in the province of Galilee, and the house and room where Our lady dwells.

Later, Ignatius adds:

> First I will see all the different people on the face
> of the earth, so varied in dress and behavior. Some
> are white and others black; some at peace and oth-
> ers at war; some weeping and others laughing; some
> well and others sick; some being born and others
> dying, etc.

At times, Ignatius progressively focuses in on the
subject of his meditation like the zoom lens of a movie
camera; at other times he seems to pull back and focus
on the larger picture. The key is to feel free to visualize the characters and scenes in these meditations in
whatever way most comfortably helps you feel con-
nected to the subject of each exercise.

To facilitate your own mental representation of
place, you can read these meditations in a number of
ways. One good approach is to record the meditation
first on a small cassette or microcassette recorder and
let it play back as you listen with eyes closed. If you
don't have a recorder handy or don't like using one,
you can read the entire meditation to yourself, close
your eyes, and visualize the scene you have just read.
You can also read one line or one paragraph at a time,
closing your eyes and letting the scene take shape grad-
ually in your mind before you go on to the next. In all
cases, as you sit calmly with eyes closed, allow yourself to see and hear the setting and characters, feeling

and smelling the warm air or sea breeze, hearing the sounds of the ancient countryside or city as you imagine them. Let your meditation focus as concretely as possible on the individual speaking, allowing yourself to create a face and costume. Historical accuracy isn't important; just try to get a visual sense of the person speaking.

As much as possible, allow yourself to feel the dominant emotion of the meditation, whether it is love, tenderness, skepticism, fear, anger, or outrage. Don't tell yourself that this is foolish or that you would never talk in such a way. We have all felt these emotions at one time or another, even if we prefer to think that we haven't. You may be comfortable with Christ's teachings, but you might respond with anger or suspicion to someone teaching a different religion or a different approach to spiritual practice—perhaps even this one. Allow those feelings to surface without judging them. And if you feel drawn to one particular phrase or sentence in the meditation, allow yourself to stay there for a while, because it is probably significant for you. When you have finished and you feel the images fading, rest in the knowledge that the Holy Spirit is working within you to heal the particular emotion addressed by the meditation.

I have arranged the meditations into sections based loosely around which emotions they will be most helpful in healing or celebrating. As a way of easing into the more challenging meditations, I have begun with a series of celebrations of the love and friendship that Jesus must have induced in many of those coming near him. As difficult as those times were, with a foreign army occupying the land, with fear and mistrust and mental imbalance rampant, the powerful force field of Jesus was still able to calm troubled vibrations around him and generate loving feelings in those who were open to him.

CELEBRATING
LOVE
and
FRIENDSHIP

⊸ *Mary Magdalene* ⊸

Jesus was a man I loved, a man I could feel tender with, talk to, and understand. He was a flesh-and-blood man who understood the feelings that can lift you up or knock you down. Although he became my spiritual master, my first memory of him was how tall he looked and how he stood out among those hypocrites who wanted to stone me to death because I needed someone to love, someone to touch and hold me close, to rid me of my loneliness. Do you know what a living hell it is to be alone, with no one to share your life? Jesus came over to me and looked at me gently, with compassion and tenderness, and then he asked those men how innocent they were before they tossed that first stone at me. Seems they were all guilty of something. In that moment, I discovered what love was all about, how people who love share with each other, and don't use each other.

Afterward, Jesus talked to me about life and its sweetness and joys. What he said was beautiful, and so was my newfound life of love for everyone, including the man who made it all possible. I had never been so happy, so overjoyed, exuberant, and enthusiastic about living. I wanted to sing and dance, whistle and shout, "Hey, world, look at me! I'm in love, real love!"

To be around Jesus made me different. I felt empty when he was away and when I couldn't touch him or tell him how I cared about him, because he cared about me. How devastated I was when they killed him by brutally nailing him to a cross.

But this glorious morning as I stand before his empty tomb, I can almost hear him say, "Mary," as he often did so softly, so sweetly. I know deep within me that he's alive. If only I could embrace him physically! But I feel it's not the time just yet. For now, I will be content with the knowledge that his spirit and mine are already one.

~ David, a Lover ~

How often, my dearest, I thought I knew the meaning of love. When I sought only after physical passion, only after sexual ecstasy, I had no thought of sweetness or tenderness, no thought of the loving God who brought two hearts together into one. Yet now my cup overflows with the goodness and joys of this heaven on earth, this beginning of the eternal.

My dearest lover, to know you and to know of Jesus makes my heart dance with gladness as the buttercups and lilies of the field dance to the music of a soft summer breeze blowing gently over the verdant meadows. When I first heard those words of kindness and understanding flow from his mouth as the living waters of a small creek gracefully winds down a mountainside, I knew I had glimpsed the mystery of the universe. Love filled him and moved him and was his reason for being here among us. Love, the secret of the ages, was no secret at all to him.

I felt love for this man like no other. Because of his teachings, now I know the meaning of life. And I can expand that meaning to encompass you totally, for you are my world, my other self, the dwelling place of God made flesh. To embrace you is to embrace the Lord. To hold you close makes me feel united with God in one flesh. Talking to you, I talk to God. Being tender with you, I am able in many ways to experience the Kingdom within. Jesus has taught me to see you, my beloved, as my lesson in joy. Uniting in oneness with you, I have met the Universe and floated with the stars.

Andrew, Peter's Brother

Simon Peter and I were fishing one day by the Sea of Galilee when Jesus came walking along the beach smiling. He beckoned us from the boat, and we laid down our nets to see what he wanted. We talked about fishing, boating, and how hard life was for the people of our land. Then, Jesus paused for a moment, gazed softly into my eyes, and asked, "Would you like to be a fisher of men, teaching them the true meaning of the good life?"

I hardly understood its meaning myself, but I quickly accepted this man's challenge. My job had begun to feel routine, and I needed a change, a chance to find out more about myself and life. We walked the length of the beach discussing truth and joy. I experienced something I hadn't experienced for years, maybe for my entire life. I experienced an honest relationship with another person—a person I could call "friend."

In years past, I had avoided close relationships because I feared people. I feared what they thought of me, what they thought of others, what they thought, period. But now I felt a change of heart, thanks to Jesus. His words lifted me up to a point where I could trust again. I could trust not only others but also myself. To be his disciple was an honor for me, a glorious honor.

Peter

Sitting in this boat today, on my way to another part of the world to preach the wisdom of Jesus, I watch the gentle flow of the water serenely passing by, and it makes me think of those glorious moments I spent with him. Being in his presence was like being in a meadow on a warm, summer morning when the air is fresh and the sky is a magnificent blue, or like being on a lake when the water is peaceful. Whenever I was with him, I felt so uplifted, so free.

And yet thinking of Jesus also brings back bitter memories of the night I denied him three times after he was led away to be put to death. I wanted to do everything right, yet fear was buried deep within me, insecurities that clouded my thinking with concerns about what others might say when they found out that I was Jesus' disciple and friend. What would they do to me? Would they kill me, too? Would they force me into exile? I had few friends, and I didn't want to lose them, yet I turned my back on my greatest friend. O God, if I could only forget that depressing, haunting, dark memory. It seems to affect everything I do. It seems to affect the way I feel about myself. God, can't I ever do anything right? What do people expect of me? What do they want from me?

That's funny. I just thought of something I never thought of before: What do I expect of me? What do I want from myself? For one thing, I want to be free. I want to enjoy the abundant life Jesus spoke about. I want to celebrate life, to feel it flow powerfully through my very being.

Thinking back to the day I first met Jesus, I can remember how I felt before he appeared on the shore. I was wondering if my life would ever be easy, instead of one long struggle to make ends meet. I was telling myself to stop daydreaming and get back to my fishing or we wouldn't have anything to eat. And then I heard a great commotion coming from the shore. I wondered, *What is John yelling? I'll row closer to the shoreline and see for myself.* I think I can make out John's words now, something about—no, it can't be. This is a dream. It's not possible. The Messiah? Can it really be? I'm not taking any chances. I'm going to get out of this boat right now and swim to the beach!

Jesus, it is you! I'll get my net full of fish and bring them here for you to put on the charcoal fire. You are getting ready to say something. What? You ask me if I love you. Of course, I do, yet why can't I say it? Why do I feel empty again? Why is my stomach whirling around like a pinwheel? "Yes, Jesus, I think a lot of you." Those words don't satisfy me. What's wrong with me? The right words won't come out.

No, Jesus, I can't feed your sheep. I have nothing to give them but bitterness, bad memories, unforgiveness. No, Jesus, why do you ask me again if I love you?

I can't face you, nor do I wish to recall the events that led to your horrible death. Maybe it would be best, Jesus, if you just left me alone and let me take my place with all the other sinners.

Oh, your eyes, Jesus, they are telling me that . . . could it be? I'm forgiven, I'm loved, I'm a new person. I have something to give to others. Can this memory be healed and never have the power to hurt me again? Will the sting be gone when I think of my betrayal of you? Is it true? Yes, Lord, I'll face it. I'll let it go into your hands. Yes, Lord, I want healing. I want to be whole. Yes, Lord, I want to be a solid rock the way you see me, not the way I see myself, a reed blowing in the wind, not knowing which way to go. Yes, Lord, I love you. Yes, Lord, I will feed your sheep, because now I have something to give them: MYSELF!

Thank you for believing in me so that I can believe in myself. Thank you for loving me so that I can love myself and give myself lovingly to others. Yes, Lord, I will go where you want me to go. Yes, Lord, I love you. You know that I love you.

Johanna,
a Child's Mother

It was spring, and the warm air was gently blowing through the Kidron Valley, a favorite spot of the Nazarene. He used to sit near the lake on one of those huge rocks that protrude by the shore. Mothers would bring their children to see Jesus, to talk to him, and to be blessed by him. He had such a wonderful way with children. He was so affectionate, so full of understanding and a delightful sense of humor, something often lacking in our own teachers of religion. My little boy had often asked me to take him to see the joyful man about whom the other children spoke. I, too, was curious about this man who healed others, and so with my boy I walked the short distance to the valley where he taught. When we arrived, we saw many children near Jesus. He was talking with them about the Father's love for all of us, but especially for children. When he spoke of the Lord, he called him "Daddy," as if the Lord were a loving Father and not a righteous, vengeful God.

A spirit of friendliness and gaiety filled the air, until one of Jesus' disciples became angry and began to send the children away. He said that they were taking up too much valuable time, which Jesus needed to teach the adults. Suddenly, Jesus stood up and in a firm tone said,

"Let the children be. They are hurting no one. Besides, you might take a lesson from them. Notice their joy, their sincerity, their sense of humor, their gratitude, and their love. Unless you become as they are, your chances of being filled with the Kingdom—that state of inner peace I have been telling you about—are rare indeed."

There was silence except for the children, who were off to one side singing love songs to God. What a lesson Jesus taught us that day! To be sure, it stung our hearts at first, especially the heart of that disciple who had pushed the children away from Jesus. Shame was written all over him, yet Jesus still looked at him with love.

Then Jesus took my little boy and placed him on his lap. He put his hand on my boy's head and smiled. Looking my way, Jesus said, "He is a good boy, Johanna. He will do much good someday. Take pride in him. He is God's own child." With that, the Nazarene returned my boy to me and walked toward the lake with his disciples until they disappeared on the other side. It was spring, and the sun was setting, casting a beautiful array of colors across the Sea of Galilee.

John,
the Beloved Disciple

My life never seemed darker than that day when I sat alone near the Sea of Galilee, throwing pebbles into the water. I had no one to talk to, no one to trust, no one to care about, and no one to care about me. *Why did I ever leave home?* I wondered. Was it really that rough, all that fighting, arguing, and discontent filling the air like a forbidding storm? I had to admit that it was, and that I couldn't take it anymore. There had to be more to life, and I had to seek it on my own. I had to find myself, but where could I go? To whom could I turn? O God, how I needed a friend.

Could you hear me, Lord, a young man calling out to you in his desperate hour of need? Would you give me someone, anyone, to love and love me in return? How bleak everything looked to me. No hope, no future, no life. I threw a rock into the water, then another and another to pass the time as I waited alone for an answer. I didn't notice the silent figure of a man approach my side and stand over me as a protective father stands over his young. I never even felt his presence, so engrossed was I in the ripples caused by the rocks striking the water. Then I heard his voice for the first time—a voice full of tenderness and compassion, unlike any I had ever heard before. I looked up at this tall man and saw affection and love in his eyes. My heart jumped with joy. *God,* I thought, *could this be the friend for whom I prayed?*

I remember the scene as if it were yesterday. He sat down beside me, placed his hand on my shoulder, and asked me who I was. "I am called John," I said.

"That's a fine name," he said. "They call me Jesus."

Suddenly, without any doubt or hesitation, I knew that this man was God's gift to me, the answer to my prayers. God had heard me and sent me a friend. I took him by the hand as we both stood up. My troubles and loneliness had vanished. My heart was filled with gladness as I watched him smile and listened to his laugh. He was no ordinary man, this new friend. He was filled with the kindness and love of God himself. He asked me to accompany him on his journey up and down the countryside, telling everyone the good news of God's love, and without even thinking, I accepted.

A new day had dawned for me. The sun never seemed brighter, the sky never a more peaceful shade of blue. Even the flowers seemed ready to burst from the ground in joy to thank the living Lord for my new love. What a glorious day it was, that day when my new life began, thanks to the Light that brightened my darkness!

I love him more than life itself, because he is my life. His light has shown me a life I never knew existed. Jesus, I've never loved anyone more than you.

You cared for me when nobody else seemed to care. You weren't afraid to put your arms around me and show me the affection I longed for even when others seemed to misunderstand your motives. I will never forget your tenderness. Thanks, my dearest friend, thanks.

Jason, a Shepherd

I was there when Jesus spoke about the good shepherd. How great it was to hear a religious master speak so admiringly of such a humble job as mine. Everyone listened to each word as he spoke: "I am the good shepherd who protects his sheep from those who rob one of inner peace and happiness. I am not fearful or weak but courageous and strong, for the life of my sheep means much to me."

He spoke of shepherds as if they were leaders of men, ready to teach others life's meaning.

"I came so that you might have life and have it abundantly. Because of this, I am the good shepherd who rids himself of all notions of selfishness and greed and teaches others to do the same. I will never abandon my sheep any more than the courageous shepherd would. I am concerned about my sheep, and we know each other on a very personal basis. We are one with God because we love."

Some were angered by his words for they think of sheep as only dumb, smelly creatures. They do not see a sheep's beauty and simplicity as Jesus did. His words brought me joy, and I loved him for it.

Nathaniel,
~ *a Fisherman* ~

I knew that Jesus loved nature, because he spent so much time by the seashore, watching the gulls fly over the water in search of food. He'd gently place his foot into the sparkling water to feel refreshed. Children playing nearby would run over to him, and he would put his arms around them and playfully joke with them. Yes, the children loved this warm, humble man who sat by the seashore. Sometimes he would teach them the joys of living, helping them discover the beauty inherent in the sunset, the clean water, the smooth dive of a gull, even the beauty one human could find in another. Sometimes he sang to the children while they clapped their hands, keeping tempo with his song of joy.

On occasion, he would tell us where to throw our nets for a catch, and it was uncanny how many more fish we caught whenever we followed his advice. And when the catch was brought in, he would help clean and cook the fish himself, and nobody was better at it. You'd think he had grown up a fisherman, not a carpenter. He was not a selfish man, always willing to share his knowledge, wisdom, and skills with us, the fishermen of this little village. He was a good neighbor who enjoyed moments with his friends, while at other times he preferred to hike up into the mountains to pray and meditate by himself. Never moody but sometimes sad, he always had a kind word for us all.

We loved him so, this gentle human being, this man who saw in Nature's perfection the beauty of his God. He was a real man to me—one like I wanted to be. We became friends, and that fact alone will always be one of my greatest riches!

~ Zechariah, an Innkeeper ~

As long as I live, I will never forget that evening when his disciples came to my inn. They wanted to use my dining room to celebrate the Passover. It was an honor for me, for I had heard Jesus speak, and his words struck my heart with such force that they dissolved its hardness forever. Never again would my spirit be darkened by negative thoughts, fears, or doubts. Never again would I permit myself to slip headlong into a deep, inescapable rut. Jesus had set me free with his teachings of love. I no longer wished to be held in bondage by desires, thoughts, and feelings that impeded my growth to such a degree that I was no longer human. Jesus was so human; he knew my feelings, and he touched me. I knew what it meant to love and be loved in return. Jesus was human, and he displayed all the emotions of a human.

That night he ate here with his friends. He had a look in his eyes of foreboding—not fear, but more like sadness—yet he was not tense or uneasy. He thanked me for all the preparations I had made in my small but comfortable upper room, letting me know that he appreciated what others did for him. Jesus always spoke words of gratitude.

I'm glad he used my inn. I shall always be grateful for those few precious hours I was able to spend in his presence. But I shall miss him. Yes, I shall miss him.

HEALING ANGER, SKEPTICISM, and SELF-DOUBT

John the Baptist

Jesus of Nazareth was my cousin. He was unlike any other man I ever knew—kind and considerate, so loving and full of compassion that the people were astonished. At times, some of them felt as if we were perpetrating a hoax—that I was telling everyone that Jesus was the Messiah, and he was acting as if he were the only child of God. They never understood what he was trying to do. They called us liars, charlatans, and magicians, but we weren't any of these things. We were only trying to teach people how to find happiness, how to connect with God. But they couldn't understand because they had been living in ignorance for so long that the Truth had evaded them. They hated us for teaching love and the fullness of life.

I told the people to change their thinking and turn back to God and find joy and meaning in Him. They misunderstood and chose to ignore me. As my sign of new life, I used the clear, sparkling water that flows in the river Jordan, but they scoffed because they did not understand. They could not see the beauty in the water, symbol of cleanliness, of a new and free spirit. They could not see that in each rainfall God cleansed the flowers. They could not see the gentleness of God as He stretched forth His hands and spread the soft morning dew over the land. They could not see the cleansing power of God in the melting snows and clear running brooks. They could not see the water as the Spirit of Life, free as the gulls in the sky, refreshing body and soul. But Jesus could. He loved all of nature. He saw it as his Father's handiwork and wanted us to enjoy it in the same way. I loved him for that and he knew it. His smile told me so.

The day I baptized Jesus in the river Jordan, I felt a bolt of lightning energy charge through me. I felt the warmth and saw the light surrounding Jesus. Just being next to him, I felt the heavenly breeze of his enlightenment, as the skies opened and the Spirit of the Lord rained down on Jesus. For me, it was enough to bask in the reflected light of his glory.

Matthew,
the Tax Collector

There I sat so pompous, the envy of all the countrymen who knew how seriously I treated my job. It was my sacred duty to fleece the people of their earnings for the Roman treasury. I was robbing my own people to help the occupying army of Romans—could anything be lower on this earth? And yet I clung to the job because it was one of the few that paid a decent wage in this poor land. Full of bitterness, disillusion, and anger, I attempted to hide from my own duplicity, and the thought of such hypocrisy ate away at me internally.

Yes, the people feared me, but they neither respected nor loved me. I had no real friends, for none felt they could trust me. With no one to turn to, I had to be devoted to this work because I had nothing else. I dreaded each new day that brought with it the unbearable panic of loneliness. But this one day was different. Jesus of Nazareth passed by me. He stopped at my collection table, looked at me, and smiled! I was astonished that another Jew would treat me with respect. This holy man—some called him prophet—smiled at me so sincerely, as if he did not hold my work against me.

My heart leaped within my chest at this great sign of affection. He was willing to overlook the things I had done in the past. He saw in me some good, some redeeming point, some value. I can even recall my shock when he bent his head toward me and said, "You're called Matthew, aren't you?"

I nodded.

"Won't you come with me? I have need of your talents."

I couldn't imagine which talents he meant, but I also had no need to think it over. This was what I had been waiting for—someone who would help me feel worthwhile. Someone who needed me. Even better, someone who could give me joy. I left my past behind me with no regrets and followed the Teacher.

Thomas,
~ the Doubter ~

They told me that he'd be here tonight, dead yet alive. How can that be? It's impossible! He did say that he would transcend death, but I don't see how. Oh, well, I'm sure he won't show up—or will he? Everyone seems so calm tonight. Look at Peter and James over there in the corner talking with John. They act as if they've seen him. If only it could be true, I would sacrifice everything I have. I've been so mixed up lately, turning here and there, searching everywhere for truth, looking for an answer, any answer. My spirit is troubled. I'm afraid—afraid that it was all in vain. Why am I the only one who's miserable? The others seem so happy, so tranquil, and here I am far from being at peace. If they were telling the truth, why isn't he here yet?

Maybe he won't come because I'm here. He always felt that I was too negative, full of doubts, full of fears. He used to say to me, "Thomas, you've got to smile more. Enjoy life. Set your sights on what is good, and forget the bad once in a while. You've got to learn to live, Thomas."

His face used to light up so when he said those words. Oh, how I miss his words, his looks, his friendly attitude. I wanted that kind of joy so much in my own life, but I didn't succeed. I guess that was my big problem—I said "can't" and "don't" and "couldn't" so often that I began to believe it. That's the kind of attitude I have to change to find complete joy. That's what he was trying to tell me when he said, "Change your thinking, Thomas. Look for the sun. Even when the sun goes behind a cloud, it's still shining. You just can't see it for the moment."

Why couldn't I grasp that while he was alive? Jesus, I'm sorry I didn't believe in the good with all my heart. I'm sorry that I was so full of doubts and fears that I neglected the joy of friendship and all the good that's around me. How stupid I was! Can you forgive me? I'm really sorry.

Even as I think that, I can feel the electricity in the air. Jesus, you're here! You've really come! It wasn't a lie at all. Oh, my friend, you've heard my prayer and have come to give me hope. "Peace," you say. What a beautiful word, so calm, so tranquil, so filled with softness and gentleness! I understand now what it means, Jesus, to have faith in you.

"Peace." Faith in myself and my goals. "Peace." No more fears and doubts. "Peace." Now I finally know the meaning of your words: "With God, all things are possible." Thanks, Jesus, for this new opportunity to believe.

Hermos,
~ *a Physician* ~

Many of the people this Jesus healed were brought to me by the Pharisees for examination. I think they wanted me to expose him by proving that they were never really lame or blind or insane to begin with. But I had to disappoint the worthy Pharisees and report that these people had definitely been healed of their maladies. Some of them I had tried to treat myself but had given up as incurable. One I specifically recall, a man born blind, was brought to Jesus, and in typical fashion, everyone asked, "What sin did he commit to have this malady?"

I was standing nearby and thought how foolish these so-called religious people are sometimes. Jesus stared at them and boldly stated, "His blindness has nothing to do with his sins or his parents' sins. I am the light of the world and have come to open the eyes of the spiritually blind. I have come to dispel their inner darkness."

That really struck me. Inner darkness? Spiritually blind? Light of the world? With these thoughts circling through my mind, I walked toward the Sea of Galilee. Sitting down upon one of the many rocks that line the shore, I pondered what Jesus said. He did not look or act like a fanatic, nor did he seem possessed, as the Pharisees kept insisting. To me, Jesus seemed quite normal and exceptionally sincere. I really couldn't understand many of the things he said, that I won't deny. Maybe he was a prophet or even a god—I don't know.

I can tell you that he had some kind of healing power, though. Maybe it was just hypnotism, but it worked. People were cured. That man born blind got his sight back, which seemed an impossibility to me. As for Jesus, he's dead now. Some say he performed one masterpiece of a trick by rising from the grave. I don't know about that. I suppose if he had all that power, he could have done it. But, if you ask me, in all honesty, I'd have to say I just don't know.

Romulus,
a Roman Soldier

The high priest called us to the throne room that fateful evening and gave the order to arrest the Jew known as Jesus of Nazareth. I knew who Jesus was, but I failed to see what crime he had committed. Nevertheless, as a citizen of Rome and a centurion in the Roman legion stationed in Judea, I had to carry out the order. We were led to a garden at nightfall by a Zealot named Judas Iscariot, reportedly a friend and disciple of Jesus who turned traitor. It was an eerily quiet night; heavy clouds shielded the moon, and the stars were barely visible. Judas led us into the garden, then walked up to Jesus and kissed him as any friend would do. That was my signal to order the guards to take Jesus into custody. I gave the order, and I have regretted it to this day.

He did not struggle, resist, or curse us. He just stared sadly at Judas as if he truly desired to forgive him for this crime of betrayal. I stood motionless and wondered how a friend could do such a thing. Jealousy, disillusionment, and greed can make a man do strange things, but what reason could he have had to turn on a good friend who had never harmed him? His action was a heinous crime in itself; I would never want a man like that in my own legion. However, I was willing to use his services to carry out my orders to arrest Jesus of Nazareth. Jesus glanced my way as if to say that he knew I wasn't to blame, and yet I felt guilty. I could have protested to the procurator before Jesus was sent to him, but I didn't. I tried desperately to convince myself that this was my duty as a soldier—to arrest an innocent man. I tried to convince myself that he somehow posed a threat to the order of Rome, to the smooth functioning of our occupation forces over here. Yet how could I have done such a thing? I was raised to respect the law, but this man had broken no law, had advocated nothing violent, nor any sedition against Roman rule.

It's unbelievable how fast events happen. Before I knew it, the trial and execution were over, and Jesus was dead. I still feel today that I might have prevented it, if only I had tried. Then maybe I would have met Jesus as a friend instead of an enemy.

Barabbas,
~ a Robber ~

Through my dark dungeon cell, the cries of the mob echoed from wall to wall. The clamor was somewhat muted, yet I could tell they were crying for blood and death. It wasn't long after that the clack of the soldiers' boots grew louder and louder. They were heading in my direction. A Roman centurion pulled me from my cell, bound my wrists, and led me to Pilate. *This is the finish,* I thought. *No hope is left. Execution awaits me.*

Yes, I was a robber. But when you are taxed so heavily that you no longer have money for food, and are so hungry, what choice do you have but to become a thief? They also claim I'm responsible for an insurrection started in the city, and even for murder. Am I also to blame for the fact that my people are shackled with foreign chains, that we no longer control our own destiny? They might as well try me for being human!

Up the stairs to the throne room I stumbled, the cries of the mob getting louder, perspiration breaking out on my forehead, thoughts of my past flashing before me. How terrible it was to die by crucifixion! The huge doors to the courtyard balcony swung open. There was Pilate and another man. This was my first glimpse of

Jesus. He looked so pitiful, beaten, crowned with thorns, and clothed in an old purple cloak. He must have committed a hideous crime to be treated in such a manner. Maybe there was still hope for me. The mob usually releases a criminal during the Passover feast. Maybe they'll choose me and crucify this Jesus instead. Suddenly, Pilate's voice interrupted my thoughts.

"Fellow citizens, here is your King. Would you have him released?"

"No!" shouted the mob. "Kill him! Kill him!"

"But he is your King," Pilate retorted.

"We have no king but Caesar! He's a fake! Therefore, he must die."

Pilate looked confused. "On this occasion, who would you release? Your king or Barabbas?"

"Barabbas!" they shouted. I couldn't believe my ears. They wanted me released. I wasn't going to be crucified after all. It was then that I looked at Jesus, and to my surprise, he was gently smiling at me as if he knew all along that I would be released. I stood frozen to the floor, not sure if I was happy about this chain of events or not. Jesus would die in my place. I was truly a criminal, but him? He just couldn't be one. He surely didn't look like any criminal I'd ever known. I wanted to thank him so much for his gift of life, but how do you thank someone who is about to die in your place?

I glanced over at Jesus, and his eyes caught mine again. He gave a brief nod as if to reply to my wishes of thanks. I wanted so much to embrace him, but that was impossible as the soldiers began to lead Jesus away to Golgotha, the place where I was to have gone on this day. Instead, another's blood would flow down the side of Skull Hill, the blood of an innocent man, Jesus of Nazareth.

HEALING
the
SHADOW

∽⌒∽

Annas,
~ the High Priest ~

I'm so glad they decided to rid the country of this Jesus, but why must they send him to me? I cannot admit this in public, but he frightens me. What if he and his followers decide to kill me for judging him guilty? That's a chance I can't afford to take. My position as High Priest is my life. It didn't come easy, and so I can't jeopardize it. What am I going to do?

I know! When they bring Jesus before me, I'll send him to Caiphas. That will take the burden from my shoulders. We must rid ourselves of this nuisance, but I don't have to be the one who does it.

If Caiphas were in my shoes, he would do the same thing. He's one step higher up on the ladder, so let him make the decision. I will give this Jesus a sermon on the evils of blasphemy and then consider my duty finished. I will not condemn him. That way no one will be angry at me. My clever mind astounds even me.

Bring this Jesus to me now so I may question him!

Caiphas,
the High Priest

I grow weary with these radicals who pretend they are the Son of God when we, and only we, are keepers of all that is sacred. If anyone be chosen by the Lord, it is the priests. This man is a fool for disturbing the people, for removing their complacency, for destroying their apathy, for upsetting their ritual. Why must this type always be around to plague us? Why can't they leave well enough alone? They must be silenced for making themselves equal to God. It is the law of our people. Besides, he threatens our priesthood. The people follow him instead of us. We cannot have this, for we are the keepers of all that is sacred.

He may act kind, but it is just a trick to get the people on his side. No one can be that good. Some of our own priests are not that righteous. So how can an ordinary citizen be so good? Answer that, Jesus of Nazareth. Heh!

If only you would consider pleading guilty, we would forgive and forget. What do you think of that, Jesus? Are we not decent under such trying circumstances? Don't just stand there staring at me—say something!

All right, Jesus. You've had your chance. I rip my cloak as a sign of how your blasphemy offends me. There will be others like you, but we shall deal with them in the same manner. Fools like you have always existed, calling themselves prophets when only we priests are the true prophets.

But we know how to deal with your kind. You are not good for the people. You teach them things they should not know. They are better off left in ignorance. And so, unfortunately, you must die, Jesus. There is no other choice. Pilate will see it my way. Now, get out of my sight, damn you! Go plead your case before Pilate.

~ *Pontius Pilate* ~

By the gods, another troublemaker brought to me! Why don't they just shut up and stop rocking the boat. They've always got to create a name for themselves. Why don't they leave me alone? Look at him standing there before me. Why doesn't he tremble or sweat or show some sign of fear? These free spirits, they baffle me. Others literally shake in my presence, but not this one. I've got to find out why.

They say that this Jesus is a king, but he doesn't look like one. To be a king, he should look stately and royal, like me! I'm only a governor now, but I shall be king one day and then everyone will tremble. Everyone will fear me, even this Nazarene, if he should live so long. Doesn't he know that I have the power of life and death over him?

He's actually staring at me. Such audacity! He's staring as if I have no power, no authority over him at all. Yet why does he frighten me so? I do believe he scares me more than I scare him. It's not natural. Let me shout at him. He doesn't budge. He doesn't move an eyelash. He just calmly stands there staring at me. I'll shout again and threaten to have him executed. He'll give in to that. Move, damn you, move! Stop standing there as if you were an immovable statue!

I've got to find a way to force him to give in to me. I don't want to kill him, yet I must or the mob will hate me. I've got to find a way to destroy him before he destroys me. They tell me he has incited riots and destroyed public property by turning over the merchants' goods in the Temple. It seems to me that those are hardly grounds for all of this uproar by the priests. They don't fool me, though. They're afraid of him, too. He's upsetting the status quo. He's letting the people know that the priests can be hypocrites, too. The priests don't much care to have that made public knowledge.

Still, I have to go along with them or they will turn on me. As much as I hate to admit it, I need those pompous fools to keep my job. That means you'll have to recant your teachings, Jesus, or die! I'm sorry, but my hands are tied. Don't look at me like you pity me! I'm your ruler, can't you see that? I have power over you . . . I think.

At any rate, summon Justus, the cross maker, to me, at once!

Justus, a Cross Maker

Some people think that there is little call for a profession like mine, but Rome is a powerful empire with more than its share of dissidents, and because of their misdeeds, many of them have been condemned to die. Now this Jesus comes along, looking more like royalty than our Roman governor does. He stands there strong and tall, his simple white garment flowing in the breeze.

I sense from the crowd's reaction, however, that I will indeed be making another cross, for there are some who undoubtedly hate Jesus and incite others to do the same. But what exactly do they fear? I really don't know. When I first gazed upon him, he seemed harmless and innocent enough. But then, one shouldn't be causing trouble either. Besides, without criminals, there wouldn't be any need for my job, and then where would I be? I suppose it is unfortunate that a man like this, one of my people, has to die at the hands of the Romans. It also seems as if somebody should be standing up for him. When he preached in the countryside, I hear he had thousands of followers hanging on his every word. Where are they all now?

Oh, well, when you work for the government, you can't say too much or you might be the next to go.

Herod Antipas, Tetrarch of Galilee

During my tenure in Jerusalem, I heard many rumors concerning Jesus of Nazareth and his strange powers. When I first heard of his growing fame, I said to my servants that he must be John the Baptist come back from the dead. I still felt bad about having been tricked into putting the Baptist to death. But whether the tales of this Jesus were true or merely exaggerations, I wasn't much concerned. The responsibility for dealing with criminals was entrusted to the high priests and to Pilate, the Roman governor. I always tried to keep out of Jerusalem politics because I had no more use for the high priests than I did for Pilate. To me, they all had hidden agendas. Why they would get upset over some harmless magician was beyond me. How could he possibly hurt them?

My plan would have been simple enough: Ignore the fool. I'll leave you alone if you'll leave me alone. But alas, that was not my fate, thanks to that spineless Pilate and those idiots we call high priests. One night during the feast of Passover, there was a widespread rumor that Jesus was in deep trouble for upsetting the Pharisees with some kind of false teaching and preaching. I had heard of Jesus' sayings and of his tricks, and

I took them in stride. But others were not so calm about it all. Annas, the high priest, talked to Jesus, and, fearing a reprisal from the crowd, sent him to Caiphas, another high priest. Caiphas muttered some platitudes of piety, did some ritual cloak ripping, and called Jesus a blasphemer. But he, too, feared the crowds, and so he sent Jesus to Pilate.

The spineless Pilate was always fearful of anyone who might cause him to lose prestige or control. Pilate talked to Jesus and tried desperately to appease the mob. But those fools wanted blood. Pilate listened, pretending to be courageous, no doubt, and then sent Jesus to me. I was glad at first, because I wanted to see this magician do some of the tricks that had made him so famous. I could become the toast of the town if Jesus would work for me. People would flock from everywhere to the court of Herod the Magnificent. I asked him a number of questions, but he would not answer. And I asked for a demonstration of his powers, but he would not perform.

Becoming somewhat annoyed and angered by his attitude, I shouted threatening epithets at him, but he didn't budge. He wouldn't even glance at me. I am Herod! Didn't he know that? Suddenly I realized that I was getting all upset for no reason. I wanted nothing to do with Jesus, Pilate, or that unruly mob of people. Life was a party to me. Why should this man destroy it for me? I must admit that there was something about Jesus that attracted me, pushing me to find out more about him. And yet I was so disturbed at Pilate that I wanted to see how he would worm his way out of this predicament.

So I sent Jesus back to him dressed like a mock king. The last I heard, the mob got its way and Jesus was killed. That's kind of sad, though, because we could have made a good pair! I guess that's life.

Foronias,
~ *a Teacher of Religion* ~

His words startle and offend me. For years I had been a respected teacher of religious beliefs and truths. Now this upstart Jesus comes along, and instead of following the laws and rituals, proposes a new and different philosophy of love. His incessant talk of love definitely disturbs me, as if I do not understand love and all it entails.

Jesus speaks too much of the emotions when he should be more concerned about the intellect. I have heard him speak his philosophies, his interpretations of God's word. He is not right. There is only one truth, and we teachers of religion have it. It is based on law. That is the only truth. Jesus speaks of abundant life when we should all be content with our lot. If we are poor, we must remain poor. If we are called to a job, we must remain there. If we believe something to be true today, we must believe it always; we cannot keep changing what we believe. It is God's way. I, Foronias, have spoken.

This Jesus needs to be reported to our authorities, for he talks too much. Religion is a set of laws to which we must adhere if we are to deserve God's love. How dare he claim otherwise. Who ever heard of a God of love? God is just God, raining death and destruction upon those who disobey him and follow evil ways. He punishes those who break the law fiercely and without mercy. These new teachings and false interpretations of Jesus could lessen the fear of God that keeps people toeing the mark; it might release them from their chains of guilt, causing them to become free thinkers. That would create havoc and chaos, and we cannot have it.

We teachers of religion will decide what is proper thinking for the people. We do not need any new religious philosophies for the people to follow like the latest fashion. They are idiots anyway, always seeking something new when they have God's gift of tradition and ancient doctrine. What more do they need? Jesus speaks of compassion and honesty, as if compassion and honesty could keep the people under control. Who needs that?

There is no doubt about it: This Jesus must die. He's a self-styled religionist who is taking the people away from the pure religion that we practice only in the Temple. Jesus is known to cavort with sinners, prostitutes, and tax collectors, to whom he speaks of love. What kind of religious man would do this? He is a liar, a cheat, and a pervert and must be punished. His teachings must be purified to coincide with ours, or else! We must show the people what manner of fraud he really is. His talk of love and understanding makes the people weak. Our talk of firmness and punishment makes them strong. He is an evil man, this Jesus, for his false concepts of religion. We will not continue to tolerate his new way of thinking any longer. He shall be punished, and, if necessary, put to death. Then we will hear no more of him or his ghastly new religion!

— Pilate's Wife —

I had a horrifying dream of impending doom for my husband and all others involved in the death of Jesus. How I tossed and turned in my bed, full of anxiety and tension, knowing instinctively the outcome of Jesus' trial being held before my husband. I have known for a long time that Pilate is not a strong ruler, especially when it comes to making decisions that will cause his subjects anger. He fears Herod because the king does not like him and will report any deviation to the Emperor in Rome, which could cause my husband to lose his job. It is a terrible way to live, or should I say, exist?

Upon waking, I ran to the throne room to tell my husband what I had dreamed. The sense of fear that permeated my whole being was like a waking nightmare. He refused to listen to me, calling my talk "nonsense," my vision "absurd."

Where could I go? To whom could I turn? Pilate said that the crowd could be controlled and he would control it. We had nothing to fear. The high priests themselves were cowards, afraid to condemn Jesus but nevertheless wanting him to be put away for good. At first, I accepted this idea. However, deep inside my heart I knew it would be different. I knew that the high priests and Pharisees wanted Jesus to die; he was too popular, and they could not contend with his grip on the people's imagination. Their jealousy ruled their misguided hearts. I stood outside the stone pavement where all judgments are rendered by the governor. It was then that I saw Jesus for the first time, pushed to the ground by a Roman soldier. The "King of the Jews" seemed so pathetic. My heart bled for this poor man, punished for no crime on his part, but rather for the Pharisees' jealousy and hatred.

How could my husband condemn this man? I know better than anyone his faults and his penchant for cruelty, but I always believed that he had good common sense. Yet he must have felt he had no choice. Annas and Caiphas saw to that. By the gods, how did we ever get into this predicament? How can we get out of it? Jesus is not a guilty man. He is a kind man. If my husband goes through with this, how can I continue to love him? How will I be able to respect him and his governorship? I may hate him forever because of this awful deed. Pilate, you fool, listen to me before it's too late!

Rexus, a Merchant
in the Temple

That Jesus must be a madman, overthrowing those tables in the Temple! The priests let us use the Temple to sell our wares, and if they don't care, why should it matter to anyone else? He is just a rabble-rouser who wants everyone to know his name. We had a great thing going in the Temple, selling our goods for a profit. Maybe at times we interfered with the religious atmosphere, but so what? We were giving a "cut" to the priests, after all.

Now I have a horrible mess to clean up, thanks to this Jesus character. To think that he said he cared more about the Temple than we do! I resent that. I care about the Temple and its furnishings and about keeping it clean. I care about the priests doing their duty. I care about the rituals being performed correctly. I also care about paying my Temple tax on time. What more do they expect? This love of God and neighbor that Jesus is talking about is beyond me. Besides, what has that got to do with my being faithful to the Temple laws and loyal to its priests? Oh, well, I've got to clean up this area. Someday they'll get Jesus for this!

Demetrius, a Roman Silversmith

I am considered one of the best silversmiths in all of the eastern world. People flock here to see my shrines and statues made of silver. They are expensive, to say the least, but nothing is too good for those who live in the heavens. It was last spring, I recall, when Jesus and I had our argument. He wandered into my shop and commented on my craftsmanship. "Your silver work is beautiful," he told me. "But is it necessary for you to limit yourself only to shrine making?" he asked.

"Well," I said, "it's a profitable business. Everyone wants statues to remind them of the gods who live in the heavens."

"That is not necessary," Jesus said.

At this point, I became infuriated. Jesus dared to discredit our deities. I told him that he was not welcome in my shop, at any time, for this blasphemy. Besides, what if someone heard him and believed him? Where would my excellent silversmith shop be today? Of course, there's no danger in that now, for the governor saw to it that Jesus would bother no one again.

Imagine him, degrading my shrines and statues while exalting humanity and someone he called God the Father! As if flesh and blood are more important than my shrines and statues.

~ Simon the Magician ~

They told me of the miracles being performed by a Nazarene named Jesus. He could heal, walk on water, and change water into wine through some process called the Holy Spirit. I remember making the journey to Jerusalem to talk with his followers so that I might purchase these great secrets. What a fortune could be made with the secrets to Jesus' tricks, especially if they were tied to religious beliefs!

I never got to see Jesus before he was put to death, unfortunately, but I did talk with a few of his disciples. The one named Peter did all the talking, or I should say, yelling. He called me names and said that what I wanted to do was wicked and that my heart was warped. I didn't follow that line of thinking. Could Peter actually be naive enough to believe that Jesus really did what he said? Strange how this Nazarene magician managed to fool even those with whom he worked. That's a trick in itself! Well, I never did get to learn their secrets. The one called Peter wouldn't let me. I admire such loyalty. My people don't give me that kind of loyalty. There was no doubt in my mind that Jesus was the greatest in our trade. Given what he did, he must have been the best magician in all the land.

HEALING LOSS
and
DEPRESSION

Rachel,
Barabbas's Lover

I found myself in a horrible situation, loving Barabbas, the thief and murderer, but I knew no better. When they arrested him and threw him into his dungeon cell, my world seemed to collapse. What could a woman do without her lover?

At about that time, I heard tell of a man called Jesus, who was teaching nearby. With some friends, I went to hear him speak. Where else could I turn? Maybe this Jesus could lift my depression. As it turned out, he did that and more. He showed me a way of life that I had never known, a way to live completely every minute of the day and be full of joy. When I thought of my lover, Barabbas, I did not hate him for what he had done, but I also realized that there was more to living than stealing, killing, and hurting others.

Would Barabbas ever understand that? I didn't know, but I had no way of reaching him anyway, so I continued to follow Jesus until that awful day when he was arrested like a common criminal and led before Pilate. There stood my teacher, the one who had taught me how to live and who had never harmed a living thing, being sentenced to a cruel death. For what? He was a man of peace, not war. He was a man of love, not hate. He was a man full of life, not death. I could understand sentencing Barabbas to death for what he had done, but why Jesus? What was his crime?

When Pilate offered the crowd the traditional option of releasing a condemned prisoner during Passover, the crowd shouted for Barabbas and condemned Jesus to death. What injustice! They released Barabbas, but I could only pity him. I could never really call him my lover again. I know this feeling inside me was wrong, because Barabbas did not condemn Jesus. Yet every time I looked into Barabbas's eyes, it was Jesus I saw.

How can I ever forget that day? It is burned into my mind forever. Yes, Barabbas was my lover, but it was Jesus whom I really loved!

Priscilla,
a Young Girl

M y parents took me one day to hear the orator
called Jesus from the village of Nazareth. His
lean, athletic features made me more interested in him
than in what he had to say. Suddenly he looked straight
into my eyes and said, "Unless all of you become like
children, you cannot enter the kingdom." I wasn't sure
which kingdom he was talking about, since he didn't
seem rich or kingly, and I was startled to hear any adult
speak of children as if we mattered. Most adults just
push us around like insignificant pieces of property,
which is how they think of us.

But Jesus genuinely seemed to love children. He
spoke of the sincerity and openness of children, qual-
ities that most people lose later in life. He said that all
adults must always cling to these virtues. His eyes
steadily gazed into mine as if to single me out of the
crowd, or as if he knew what I was thinking. A little
while later when he had finished speaking, he walked
over to me and placed his muscular hand on my head.

"What is your name?" he asked.

"Priscilla."

He smiled and told me always to remain sincere if
I wanted to be happy. If I did, he said, it wouldn't mat-

ter what others thought of me, because I would have happiness and peace within. Even as he said those words, my heart leapt in my breast because I knew it was true.

Yet when he walked away, I felt a certain sadness, too. *Would I see him again,* I wondered? I never did, but his smile and what he said that day have been written in my heart ever since. I have tried my best to live up to his simple words of encouragement, although I haven't always been able to do so. Each time I've failed to be completely sincere, though, I later recalled what Jesus said, and set my heart again on being true to him.

They tell me now that Jesus is dead, which seems strange somehow. He looked so strong that I can't imagine how he could have died. Whenever I ask my parents about it, they tell me to be quiet and not to talk about such matters. To them, I'm still just a child, not worthy of a sincere answer. I know one thing, though. If Jesus were here today, he'd give me a straight answer!

Cleopas,
a Follower of Jesus

How ashamed I was not to have recognized my Master as we traveled the road to Emmaus together. Bartholomew and I had just heard of Jesus' death, and we were walking along the country road, speaking of Jesus and how much he meant to us. When he approached us on the road, we were so caught up in our own sorrow and confusion that we didn't even recognize him. I explained our distracted state by telling him how sad the past few days had been for us.

"What has caused your sadness?" he asked.

Astonished and then irritated at his ignorance of all that had taken place, I said, "You must be the only person in Jerusalem who hasn't heard about the terrible things that have happened."

Then he asked for an explanation, and like a fool, I gave him the whole story in detail, which took some time to tell. As I babbled on, Jesus began to speak to us with such clarity and vision regarding sacred scripture that we begged him to stay with us, but he declined, for he had much to accomplish before his return to the Father. As we sat down at the end of the day to break bread together, he gave thanks over our meal. It was at that moment that our eyes were opened and we saw his glory revealed. Jesus had indeed risen from the dead and stood before us, warming our hearts with his words.

Jesus smiled at us and even seemed to take some delight in our not recognizing him. He was not easily angered by our folly, even if he had a right to be. No sooner had we realized our mistake than Jesus seemed to disappear before our eyes, and my companion and I were left to digest the situation. Jesus was a Prophet sent to us by God, we agreed, a mighty Teacher who worked wonders and healed the sick and crazy among us. Thinking him to be the Messiah, we were shattered by his death. Could it all have been in vain? Surely there must be more to this story than a hideous death for a kind man. Many of Jesus' followers fled and fell by the wayside after the ordeal of the crucifixion. Others dispersed when they heard that his body had disappeared. We were in terror and anguish, ready to abandon him and everything for which he stood. Hopelessly dejected, we had left Jerusalem for Emmaus, and he appeared to us as if to shore up our faith. Fortified by his life and strength, we set out once again to preach Jesus' name wherever we went. Alleluia, Jesus lives in our hearts and in our thoughts!

HEALING PHYSICAL LIMITATIONS

Bartimaeus,
— a Blind Man —

I can remember quite clearly that warm afternoon when Jesus, his disciples, and a large crowd came to Jericho. I was sitting at the side of the road, begging as I had been taught to do years ago. Such a racket was being made by the mob that at first I thought it was a riot, but the people didn't seem to be full of anger, as rebellious people are. Then I thought it was the soldiers coming to arrest someone, but that couldn't be either, because a feeling of happiness filled the air, and as a rule, soldiers do not spread joy. I heard someone shouting, "Here comes Jesus! Jesus of Nazareth is coming this way."

Jesus of Nazareth, I thought. The man some call the Messiah is coming to Jericho. I must call out to him. I must stop him and talk to him. This is my chance to be healed.

"Son of David," I shouted. "Son of David, have mercy on me!"

Some people were embarrassed by my presence and tried to stop me from shouting. But I am not easily swayed, and so I shouted louder. "Son of David! Son of David, have mercy on me!"

Suddenly there was a hush, and I heard Jesus say in a calm and peaceful voice, "Call that man to me."

Overjoyed, I got up, threw off my cloak, and stumbled and fell in my joy to meet Jesus.

"What do you want from me, Bartimaeus?" Jesus asked. I was stunned that he actually knew my name. How did he find out? Who told him? Oh, that's right, this is Jesus, the prophet! I laughed so hard that tears were streaming down my eyes. What a great pleasure it was to meet Jesus. Finally, getting control of myself, I answered his question. "Please help me to see again."

"Go," he said. "Your faith has restored your eyesight."

That's all there is? I thought. Then it happened. The sunlight filtered through my eyes and slowly began to take shape, blurry at first, then clearly forming into white, billowy clouds that floated lazily across the sky. The sky! It was so glorious and blue. I remembered it from my childhood, before I went blind, but had never really hoped to see it again. Or the flowers, lovely wildflowers that grew by the roadside, a blur of color.

Slowly, people's figures and then even their faces became clear to me. In my joy, I jumped up and hugged Jesus. I was so ecstatic. He smiled and said, "Stay well and be happy, Bartimaeus, for the Father loves you."

I followed him, blending in with the crowd, and became one of his disciples. I no longer had to beg for a living, and yet I had learned no trade. Instead, I would travel the land with his followers, spreading his message and helping to heal others, depending once again on the good wishes and generosity of the people to make my living.

Alphaeus,
a Paralytic

Capernaum was my home when I met Jesus, whom my parents took me to see because of my paralytic condition. When we arrived at the home where Jesus was staying, the mob was pressing in on all sides. Sensing my disappointment and fear of missing Jesus, four of my relatives took me to the interior roof of the court area and lowered me on a stretcher directly in front of the spot where Jesus was teaching. He looked up at the unusual sight, and for a moment, a puzzled look crossed his face as he watched my pallet being lowered. When he noticed that I was clutching the ends of the stretcher in great anguish, he began to smile.

"What a unique way to enter a room," Jesus said, to the amusement of the crowd. "What is it you wish from me?" His voice was tender and affectionate.

"To be cured," I blurted out.

"So it is," he said, as if it were the simplest thing on earth. "You are made whole, and all your faults are forgiven and forgotten."

I was overjoyed. Some scribes sitting there were mumbling about the statement Jesus had made, but I didn't care because I was cured. I knew that the scribes and Pharisees were always complaining about something, so their grousing didn't bother me in the least. I also knew that Jesus was a wonderful man, not only because he helped me walk again, but also because he was loving and kind. When I began to weep from joy, he placed his arms around me and said, "Alphaeus, man can do whatever he wishes to do if he believes in himself and the Father. Don't ever forget that."

I haven't forgotten!

Flavius,

~ a Centurion's Son ~

I heard him preaching that warm, breezy summer afternoon and knew he was sent from the heavens. If only he could make me whole and heal my crippled leg! He approached the area where I was sitting. I asked him, and in a voice so deep, yet loving, he asked if I believed I could be healed.

"Yes, I do," I said.

Instantly I felt a stillness and peace come over me. Jesus smiled and said calmly, "You are healed."

What joy flooded my soul! I got up and literally danced for the first time in years. And Jesus stood there clapping out a rhythm with his hands so that I could dance more easily! Around and around I went until I fell exhausted into Jesus' waiting arms. He embraced me and held me so close.

"You are made whole in body and spirit," he whispered. "Now you will forever know the meaning of the fullness of life and abundant joy."

I have never forgotten this wonderful man from Nazareth. He walked away as I watched the afternoon sun slowly dip into the horizon and cast its rays around the figure who, at a distance, turned back and waved a friendly good-bye. The birds sang, the breeze whistled a happy tune, and his words rang within my spirit. "Ask whatever you want and believe you have it—and then it is yours."

HEALING FEAR
and
EMBARRASSMENT

⟋ Simon of Cyrene ⟍

What a terrible sight this man is crawling along the cobblestones, his knees wracked with scratches, his back bleeding profusely from the beating they have given him. And for what? I am still not able to understand what evil he has done. I'm new in town and only came out to see what the commotion was all about, but my heart goes out to this poor man. This must be the one I heard about who was dragged before Pilate, the one they call Jesus of Nazareth. From what I'm told, his great crime was to heal the sick and preach love for each other. What a radical notion!

What now? What's that Roman guard doing beckoning me to come forward? They always make trouble for us, and now I'm afraid. What, he wants me to help carry the man's cross? Wait a minute. I sympathize with this Jesus and his suffering, but really, this is too much. I don't want to get involved. What will people say? Hey, stop pushing me. I'm a man of means. You can't treat me like a slave.

I don't have any choice, though, and if I resist the soldiers' demands, they may crucify *me*! At least people won't be able to say I did this of my own accord. They will have to admit that the soldiers forced me. Oh, this beam is heavy, full of splinters and coarse, cutting edges. I can see what it has already done to this poor man's shoulders—they're ghastly! If there wasn't anyone around, I'd wipe the blood off him, but too many people are watching.

Jesus, why did you get me into this mess? How will I be able to explain this to my friends? I feel sorry for you, but this is awfully embarrassing. Hurry up, let's go before too many people see us. Oh, I'm so embarrassed.

James, an Apostle in the Garden of Gethsemane

Jesus looks so sad leaning against the rock, praying. He thinks we are all asleep, but I alone have stayed awake watching him pray while his whole being seems to be alive in another dimension. So still he kneels, unaware of my presence. I sense that something terrible is about to happen—what, I don't know. We've shared so many good times together that I can't bring myself to believe they are about to end. Maybe Jesus is so pensive this evening for another reason. Yet foreboding fills the very air surrounding us, a feeling of evil and despair about to be let loose.

Where is Judas, I wonder? All the apostles are here except him. But before I can follow this thought any further, I see Jesus coming back toward us, asking why we couldn't remain awake with him. I do not want to single myself out or show up the others by admitting that I have been awake all along, observing him. I watch as he forlornly returns to prayer.

The Garden of Gethsemane where we are gathered is such a lovely place by daylight, but it is dark and lonely at nightfall. It holds such beautiful memories of days gone by, and the air is still fragrant with the smell of olive groves with their rich fruit that will be pressed to make the finest oil. But it is hard to think of good times now, when the Master looks so downcast and solemn. Can it be that we will never hear him teach us again? O God, don't let that happen! We love him so much. Don't take him from us.

Suddenly, my thoughts are broken by the sounds of people approaching, a large gang. Judas is finally returning to us, but who are all those people with him? Some of them carry clubs and knives, like a pack of cutthroats, and there is even a Roman soldier among them. What do they want with us? My blood freezes as they pass by the sleeping forms of the other apostles and keep moving toward the spot where the Master was praying. What can they want?

O God, no! It's happening. What I feared has come upon us. They are seizing Jesus and leading him away. I should do something, but I'm petrified with fear. This is the darkest moment of my life, but I sense that even worse days are coming.

Petrus, a Friend of Thomas the Doubter

I was one of those to whom Jesus appeared after death. When he was with us, I figured him to be a great teacher, but surely not the Messiah. I was even one of those at whom he sometimes looked askance, for I often pleaded, "One more miracle, Master. Just one more and I will believe." He seemed to pity me for my lack of belief and lack of understanding. Jesus often said to me that he honestly thought there would never be an end to this doubt of mine until I changed my attitudes. One more miracle would be an endless excuse for my disbelief and tumultuous doubts.

Jesus surely outdid himself this time, however. He has risen from the dead! At least that's what his disciples have said. Oh, surely, it is true. But maybe it's a trick to show the Romans they were wrong. I feel lost again. I need someone to talk to about this miracle, to check it out and see if it's true or not. God, if only I knew for certain. If I had just one more miracle, then I could be sure, couldn't I?

Joseph of Arimathea

Jesus was not a personal friend of mine, but you could say he was my teacher, my spiritual physician, and helper. I usually saw him only at a distance, as he was surrounded by crowds wherever he went. Everyone wanted to touch him, speak to him, and ask for personal favors. I wanted only to watch, observe, and think. What he said seemed so new, so different, so revolutionary, and yet it made sense. Even the uneducated could understand this man's teachings. I was surprised at how many enemies he made just by teaching people love and brotherhood. Maybe they chose to rid themselves of him by murder rather than admit that their own thinking was faulty.

I watched his trial before Pilate and prayed that I could be strong, like he was. While fear engulfed my being, Jesus seemed to be growing stronger, although he was the one on trial. I couldn't help noticing the contrast between Jesus and Pilate. The governor was becoming a mass of confusion and anxiety even as Jesus grew calm and serene. Jesus said little in his defense, and this, too, seemed to disturb Pilate, who wanted tangible evidence before passing sentence. In the midst of all this turmoil, Jesus stood tall among the others.

Even on the cross, he towered over the rest of us, begging us to love, forgive, and grow. Only a man of

God could do such a thing. I marveled and secretly wished I had known him better. One last gesture I was able to perform was to bury my teacher, an act that I considered an honor. As I took him from the cross, his face beamed radiantly, as if whispering to me, "I have conquered death, Joseph. No longer will it have any hold over us."

How small my fears seemed compared to his courage in the face of death.

HEALING GUILT

and

DESPAIR

⸺ Judas ⸻

What have I done to my friend? Whatever possessed me to turn from him as a lover betrays his beloved? When we began, I loved him dearly and he called me a friend. Was it greed that turned me against him and made me discard my greatest opportunity for happiness in life? Or was it my disillusionment that he was not the political leader I had hoped for? It hardly matters now, because no reason could be enough to betray a friend.

All beauty has left my life. Everything that was sweet has turned sour. That which was straight has been made crooked. Whatever was once bright has slowly dulled into eternal darkness. My God, what have I done?

Jesus and I often spent hours talking about God and his goodness, and yet all I could think about was getting more money and possessions, not realizing that possessions aren't everything—love is what really matters. I beg forgiveness for this awful deed. I need forgiveness for this dastardly deed. I deserve to be destroyed, for inside I no longer exist. I am empty, alone, despised, hated.

My world has collapsed and disintegrated, for without a lover, what is the life of the beloved worth? Without a friend, who is left to embrace? I've lost everything for one moment of selfishness. I don't believe I can ever be worthy of forgiveness. I must make my penance the only way I am able. This money they gave me is worthless. I might as well give it back to those leeches who put me up to this.

Paulenus, a Roman Citizen
~ at the Way of the Cross ~

Kill him! Kill him! He's a traitor to the people. He pretended to be like the gods, even greater than Jupiter! Therefore, he should be condemned to death. Who does he think he is, anyway? That's it, Pilate, put him to death! Hey, why are you washing your hands, Pilate? You condemned him justly. Oh, it must be some kind of ritual. Yeah, that's what it is, a ritual. Away with him. Put that cross on his shoulders, and let us get on with it.

This crowd is getting too pushy. I have to get closer to the road so I can get a good view of this madman, this pretender to the throne of Jupiter. This is one show I'm not going to miss. I'm going all the way to Golgotha to make sure I see it all. Hey, look at that! The new Jupiter fell down. Ha! What a laugh! If he really is so great, why doesn't he just fly away instead of suffering all this humiliation?

Hit him! Hit him with your whips, you stupid guards. I want to see how "Jupiter" reacts to that. Don't let him sit there. Pick him up. We don't have all day. Look at that. Jesus and his mother. She shouldn't be allowed here with all these dirty words and such foul language. What? Why am I feeling sorry for her? Well, it's not her fault that her son turned out like he did. Come on, Mary, get away from him! You can't do any more for him. He made his bed, now let him lie in it. Hey, you guys, be gentle with her—she's a lady.

It seems like Jesus is getting weaker. I guess that's why the guards are pulling that man out of the crowd. He's picking up the bottom beam and helping Jesus carry it. That's nice of him, seeing as how the guards didn't give him any choice in the matter. Ha! Now some lady is pushing her way into that mob with a cloth. Oh, I see, she's wiping off the convict's face. I heard that the women chased after Jesus because he was so gentle. That's no way for a man to act anyway, if he really is a man. After all, we men are strong, courageous, and powerful. Tenderness and compassion have no place in a man.

There he goes again, falling down. Why don't they help him up instead of kicking him when he's down? That's not right. Even if a person deserves it, you shouldn't kick him when he's down. All right, he's up again. Now he's talking to that small group of people on the other side of the road. He's smiling at them as if he's trying to comfort them. Oh, he must be mad. I can't understand that. He's putting his hand on that little boy's head and whispering to him. The boy is drying his tears and trying to smile! I don't get it. He's turning this way now. He's looking at—he's looking at ME! Oh, the poor man, he's fallen again.

Look at his eyes. He's no madman. He has such a kind face. He can't be a madman. But he can't be God either. He just can't be! But why did Pilate wash his hands? I don't understand that at all. Was he afraid? But afraid of whom? This man or the crowd? Maybe Pilate isn't the brave, courageous man I thought he was. Maybe . . . oh, that's silly. Pilate is our governor, so he must be brave. Oh, I've got to stop thinking this way. This man is guilty, and that's all there is to it.

Yet I can't help feeling sorry for him. I don't know why, but I do. He looks so innocent standing there while they strip him of his clothes, like a lamb going to slaughter. I can't bear to watch this anymore. The sound of those hammers, his flesh being torn by the nails. But he doesn't yell out. How can he remain silent? I can't stand it. I'm leaving before he dies. I think that Pilate has definitely gone too far this time. Killing an innocent man, one whose only crime was to pretend he was the Son of God. Even acknowledging that absurd claim, what evil has he done? I'm told that his words have helped people, made them happier, and that he actually healed some of them of their insanity.

Now he's saying something up there. Oh, it can't be. He's asking God to forgive us because we don't know what we are doing. This is unbelievable. He's forgiving us? I wish I had never come out to see this horrible thing today. I just want to run and hide and forget this terrible incident if that's at all possible. O Jupiter, help me. Help me forget. Help me to forgive myself.

Claudius, a Roman Soldier
~ at the Crucifixion ~

I have always disliked this job, watching men die in anguish, hanging there unable to breathe until they finally suffocate. It is an unsightly, merciless death for any man. But this man showed no fear, no despair; he looked more like one experiencing a peaceful fulfillment of destiny. I don't understand how he could accept his fate so peacefully. What has he really done? What am I doing here pounding these nails into the soft flesh of a man who has done no wrong except to teach people about love and the meaning of life? Is this a crime? Why am I doing this to him? What has he done to die so horribly, so inhumanely?

A week ago, the people cheered him when he came to town riding that donkey. They shouted, "Hosanna!" and called him king. Now this—what an end for a man, let alone a king. No more cheers now, Jesus, just jeers—jeers from the very people you said you only wanted to help. They've turned on you like hungry dogs turning on a young fawn to rip it apart. I can't help but feel sorry for you, Jesus, with these huge nails ripping your flesh, tearing at your wrists as they lift that beam higher and higher under the blackening sky. But am I any better than they are?

Look at those storm clouds gathering. We're really in for it now. I hear peals of thunder in the distance and glimpse flashes of lightning streaking across the ever-darkening sky.

What's that, Jesus? You're saying something, but I don't understand what you mean. You're talking to that young man and woman on my left, something about "son" and "mother." How astonishing! A man is dying on a cross, yet he is concerned about other human beings. And now you're saying something about forgiveness. I don't believe my ears. How can you forgive us for what we are doing when we can't even forgive ourselves? How on earth can this be, forgiving those who are killing you? Look at that sky, it's getting darker even as your body grows weak and your spirit grows lifeless.

He seems so pitiful up there, so alone, so friendless. It's hard to believe that his only crime was to love, to love enough that others might feel alive and worthwhile. I will never understand the reasons for crucifying a man for loving unless it be the fear and jealousy some have when another becomes more popular with the people than they are. We do strange things under the guise of law and order. I must go, for the sky is getting very black. The blowing and howling winds are known to bring powerful storms this time of year. It's so dreary, as if the universe itself is saddened over the death of this man—a man in love with life, in love with people, in love with his God.

Forgive me, Jesus, for being here during these painful hours, for having been a part of this travesty. Forgive me.

HEALING
SORROW
and
GRIEF

Jacob, a Psalmist

I saw that horrible sight and cried to you, O my Lord, for the forgiveness of evil done in the name of good. Why must we annihilate what we do not understand? Why must we murder the innocent, happy feelings that lie within our being? Why must we eternally run to escape our own errors and faults? Always the scapegoat. Always blaming, never relenting. O Lord, what wickedness we have beheld this frightful day. Never must such a morning dawn again in any era of time, for we have destroyed and buried our inner joy this day.

Now we lament and are saddened. Our burden is too heavy to bear. We have removed your own gift of life. "My God, my God," he cried on the cross. "My God, my God," I cry in my fever of sorrow. "Forgive us. Forgive us for this horrible deed. Wreak not your anger and judgment upon us, O Lord."

The flowers weep. The rivers cry. The rocks tremble in sorrow as the earth swallows up God's gift to man, God's own life and joy: Jesus, the man from Nazareth.

Mary, His Mother, at the Foot of the Cross

What an unbelievable end for my son! I would never have believed that it could be this way. Had I known, I would never have given birth to him. This is so hard for me to accept, my son dying as a common criminal. God, forgive my bitterness at this moment, for this trial is so hard to bear. Flesh of my flesh, blood of my blood, hanging there so full of misery, yet loving us for being his Father's children.

I look back now to those years long ago when the angel first came to me, telling of the birth of one who would save his people from themselves. I accepted, unknowingly, and with trepidation. Joseph and I traveled, attempting to escape those who already hated my son as a mere child, slaughtering hundreds of babies out of fear that one might be a king who would usurp the throne of Herod the Great. To an unknown land we fled in a desperate attempt to escape his clutches. Later we returned when Herod was no longer a threat to our child's safety.

O God, I prayed, how much more of this will I be able to handle? But Jesus was a good boy and a wonderful son who taught us much about God and life. Joseph and I didn't have all of the answers, but in the fullness of time, Jesus gave us the answers we sought. Many think as we did that a child has little or nothing to offer adults, but how false and foolish those thoughts are. A child's sincerity and affection are in themselves examples of what we can learn from them, because with age, sincerity and affection tend to harden. Thoughts such as these cause me concern regarding today's events, and I can only ponder again the tormenting question that invades and dominates my mind: *Why did this happen?* My son is guilty only of teaching human love to people afraid of love and trying desperately to shun the good within themselves.

Prior to Jesus' birth, the angel said to me, "He shall be called Emmanuel," which means "God with us." Now that he is gone, how will God be with us? Forgive me, Father, but this is the talk of a heartbroken mother. I know you will find a way. I will wait and soothe my bitter tears, waiting for your answer.

HEALING
INTOLERANCE

Crispus, a Gentile

O ur people were not considered religious because we did not follow Jewish laws and customs. Many Jews did not associate with us because of this. Yet Jesus was different; religion, nationality, race, even gender meant nothing to him. He was concerned with the internal person, not what was outside. Jesus was not known for approaching someone and asking whether or not that person was Jewish. He considered no one above him or below him because he felt that all people could benefit from his teachings. Distinctions create problems, and Jesus knew this well. "If you are tired and weary," he would say, "come to me and I'll give your mind rest."

We were thrilled that he loved us enough to include us as his followers without making us feel like outsiders, unwanted and uncared for. Jesus would willingly embrace us, and we loved him for it. His religious beliefs were true and honest, worthy of many, many followers—Jews and Gentiles alike.

CELEBRATING
WORK

Dionysus,
a Winemaker

Pressing the grapes for their juice was just a job for me—a rather tedious duty, I might add. Every day I worked in my vineyards, then gathered the grapes and took them to the winepress. I learned the work from my father and did my job diligently. It paid well, but I personally had little taste for wine and didn't really see the point of all this toil. Then one day in the vineyard as I was gathering my precious commodity, Jesus the Nazarene walked up to me. He smiled and asked if I grew these grapes. I said that I did.

"They are juicy and quite delicious," he said as he tasted one of my grapes. "You must be a very good winemaker."

Immediately my heart swelled at the thought that someone saw meaning and beauty in my work, something I wasn't able to see myself.

"Would you like some to take with you on your journey?" I asked.

"Yes, my friend," said the Nazarene. "They will refresh me and keep me from getting thirsty."

Jesus took the grapes and went on his way, leaving me whistling a happy tune. Suddenly, I realized what had happened. Jesus had seen me, a simple winemaker, as a useful person, a man whose life had meaning, an individual who could take pride in what he was doing. I was pleased. He had made me see a new side of myself, a worthwhile side. For that visit from Jesus I shall always be grateful. He helped me to live again by showing me the value of my work. What a glorious feeling! Yes, I shall always be grateful.

Abraham,
a Jewish Nobleman

Jesus was an eloquent orator whose simplicity and honesty shone through his teachings. He made no pretense at scholarship, but spoke only from the heart with a great deal of common sense. When I first heard him speak, he astounded me, since I had heard so many false rumors being spread about him. For a long time I had not wanted to hear him, because I had been told that he despised the rich. This was not the case. Jesus loved everyone. Indeed, he even said that he had come so that we might live more abundantly. Being rich was no crime, no sin. It was what we did with our riches that determined our right or wrong use of God's gifts.

After listening to Jesus speak, I learned to love him. He was a real man full of good and truth, with no pretense. Even with all my riches and my high office, I felt that life was passing me by. I was considered a learned man, yet in the practicalities of life, I was ignorant. Jesus pointed that out to me one evening when he asked me if I desired more out of life. He told me to see the beauty of everything around me, to meditate on the morning sunrise and see it as God's daily greeting. Even the flowers displayed a beauty that I had previously overlooked in all my haste to be successful.

Riches no longer are an object in themselves, but rather a guide to a loving God who grants me abundance because I know how to use and enjoy it. Although I was never a selfish person, through association and pressures I could easily learn to be. However, Jesus made the difference.

CELEBRATING FAITH

~ The Canaanite Woman ~

Why is this happening to my little girl? Why should she have to suffer so? They told me to come here and find Jesus, that he could heal my daughter. I hope they are right, because I don't know what else to do. I have nowhere to turn. Ah, there he is now. I'll go and talk to him, and plead with him to heal my little girl.

"Lord, Son of David, have mercy on me. My daughter is suffering terribly from some illness. Lord, do you hear me? Did you hear what I said?"

Why does he just stand there, saying nothing? This is so embarrassing. I keep calling out to him, and he does not answer. Even his disciples are growing weary of me. They want him to send me away. I'm getting angry at him for not answering me. Why is he doing that? I almost think he is keeping silent on purpose. Yet he is looking at me, as if he's about to say something.

What? What does he mean that he was sent only to the lost sheep of Israel? What about me? Sure, I'm no Israelite, but I need help just like they do. I feel lost. Help me, won't you Lord? Won't you help me?

He's reaching out a hand to me. I'm not the one who needs healing, Lord. It's my daughter, my little girl who is sick. Reach out to her and touch her with your healing love.

What is he saying? "It's not right to take the children's bread and toss it to the dogs." Is that what you said? I feel so hurt inside, so empty and alone, just like when I was a child and everyone around us always called our family dogs! God, it hurt so much and it still does. I resented them for treating us like dogs. I hated them so much that I could have killed them. I am not a dog—I'm a human being. Treat me like a human being, please.

Yet when I look into Jesus' eyes, I see love, respect, and kindness. He desires to treat me like a human being if I will only let him. If only I will let go of my bitterness and resentment, this hostility within me that colors and darkens everything I do. So often this hatred directed at myself destroys my relationships with the people I love the most, like my daughter. That's it! I have to let go of these negative feelings. I have to release them to this Jesus so my daughter can be healed.

Look at him smiling, as if he were reading my very thoughts. I feel such peace suddenly. I know that I've forgiven those who called me "dog," and now I am no longer condemned to live like an animal. I am forgiven even as I forgive. Thank you, Jesus. Yes, even the dogs eat the crumbs that fall from their master's table. So any crumbs you want to give me now, Lord, I will take with an attitude of gratitude.

Yes, Lord, what was that? My trust is great, and you have granted my request? Oh, thank you, Jesus, for your patient understanding and love. I love you. I love my daughter. I even love myself. Thank you. Thank you so very much!

~ *Philemon* ~

I guess you could say that I was Jesus' shadow. Until he came along, very little made sense. Don't get me wrong; life had been good to me. It just did not feel complete. There were so many contradictions, so many things I did not understand. Then Jesus came along like an answer to a prayer. I especially recall a day at the mountainside. It was late morning when the crowd finished assembling near the Lake of Galilee, a favorite spot for many because of the breeze from the sea and the beauty of the Kidron Valley itself. In the center of this picturesque setting, Jesus stood, speaking on the joy of living and prayer.

"When you pray," he said, "don't be like a hypocrite who prays only in public so others will see his pretended piety. Instead, go off by yourself. Be at peace and talk to your heavenly Father-Mother, who gives you all you need. Your Divine Parent knows your needs before you even ask. Don't recite words over and over, but talk to God as you would a friend, saying: 'My dearest Father-Mother, whose name is holy, give me your kingdom of peace, your kingdom of love, your kingdom of joy. May your will and desire for our happiness be fulfilled in our daily lives. Give us what we need to be happy, as you always do, and forgive us our faults, as we forgive ourselves as well as those who have hurt us. And deliver us from the results of worry, doubts, fears, frustrations, and all negativity.'"

The practicality and simplicity of that formula for successful living astounded me. I had never heard it so well put in all my life, to trust God to completely fill my needs because He does love me that much.

Jesus went on: "Do not worry about anything, for worry never added a day to one's life span; if anything, worry lessens the life span. Whatever you need, have faith in your heavenly Parent's love for you, and all will be given."

Then he pointed to the blue sky above, dotted with birds. "Look at the birds. They don't worry about what to eat. God in heaven takes care of them. Surely you realize that you are more valuable to God than they are?"

Jesus pointed to the flowers that surrounded each of us as we reclined on the bosom of Mother Earth, listening to his teachings. "Look at the lovely flowers that light up the countryside with their beauty and splendid array. King Solomon in all his glory was never dressed as beautifully as they. But you are more precious to your Divine Parent than these flowers."

My biggest problem has always been too little faith and trust. Jesus was such a down-to-earth man filled with common sense and practicality. He removed blinders from my eyes by his talk. His sincerity pierced my heart. I wanted to be just as he advised: free from worry, aware that God is my source of plenty—who knows my need for food, money, the good things in life—as well as beauty, nature, love, and the affection of a friend.

I was exhilarated, and Jesus knew it. Looking my way, he continued to speak as if talking directly to me. "Don't worry about tomorrow. God will take care of your tomorrow. Live one day at a time—but live fully."

HEALING
into
WHOLENESS

The Man at the Pool

My friends will be here for me in a few minutes to take me back to the pool at Bethesda. I don't really know why I bother to keep going. It has been 38 years since I first became an invalid. I can remember it so clearly. There I was, a strong young man of 20, moving that heavy stone for the Romans who were building a new viaduct. Then it slipped off its heavy rope and came tumbling forward, crushing my lower back and legs.

How I hated those Romans for what they did to me! If they hadn't made me work with that stone, I wouldn't be in this condition today. The doctors and all their medicine—no one can do anything for me. It's hopeless. I don't know why these friends of mine insist on taking me to the pool again. We were just there and nothing happened. I know about the superstition that says if I get into the pool first, immediately after an angel ripples the water, I will be healed. I think that's ridiculous, but my friends seem to believe in it. Besides, religion has never done much for me—but I promised, so I'll go.

I feel so silly, a 58-year-old man among all these hopeless people, still a cripple. Alas, it wasn't always like this! I was strong and handsome, betrothed to a beautiful woman named Claudia. Of course, she left me after the accident. Those damned Romans. I hate them all! Now my legs hang helplessly, completely useless to me. All these years of feeling nothing down there. God, do you know what it's like to feel useless, helpless, without feeling? I could scream at the futility, at not even feeling like a man! I curse the nation that did this to me.

Oh, there goes the water! Too late, someone else got there first again. This will definitely be my last trip here. This is a waste of time for me and my friends. They look at me with such pity. I hate that, too. I don't want their pity. I don't need it. Who is that man looking at me? He's smiling at me—I don't need any more pity, thank you very much. Oh no, he's coming this way. That's all I need. Another religious fanatic. What does he mean, "Do you want to be whole"? Of course I do, it's just that I can't get to the water on time.

My God, did you just hear what I said? Even I am beginning to believe those old wives' tales! That's a laugh.

"Yes, I want to be whole, no matter what it takes."

He's reaching his hand out to me. Will you look at this man's face? It's so radiant, so loving and warm. I can feel his compassion for me—not pity, but real, honest compassion and concern. He loves me!

Yes, I'll get up. Yes, I believe I can do it. I believe in you and your love. My Lord, what a terrific heat is passing through my legs and lower back! I've never felt such warmth before. Look at my legs trembling with strength! Color is coming back into them. The drab, gray skin is taking on a vibrant, ruddy hue. I have feeling back in my legs! The pain in my lower back is gone! Such peace and tranquility I have not felt in—38 years! I'm standing up now, and yet I feel as if I am about to float away on a cloud into this man's arms. How beautiful that feeling of total serenity is!

Yes, Jesus, I'm hearing you. You're telling me not to sin again by my bitter, hateful feelings and thoughts of unforgiveness. Such negativity has the power to cripple us, the power to harden us, you say, and I have to believe you. Such negativity has the power to blind us and take away our peace of mind, our joy, and our love. I realize now that my bitterness and resentment created such a negative state in me that I had no possibility of being healed.

Oh, Jesus, I promise that I will keep my thoughts positive, loving, and fruitful. I want wholeness in spirit, body, and soul. I shall remember your words always, Jesus. I shall seek after inner peace through forgiveness. I shall be all you called me to be. You have given me reason to Celebrate Life. I shall never forget! Thank you, my friend. Thank you.

HEALING OUR
IMAGE
of
GOD
and
RELIGION

Portia,
~ a Slave Girl ~

Caesar had just freed me, allowing me to leave Rome. I journeyed to Jerusalem, where everyone was talking about this man who said he was from God. This was something I had to see for myself. People told me that his talks were moving and that he uplifted the spirit and mind of everyone who heard him. Right now, my spirit seemed good, even though much of my past was spent in slavery.

I didn't want to remember the past, so I sought out this Jesus of Nazareth to see what he had to offer. He was preaching to a group of people along the Lake of Galilee when I found him. I sat down near the water and listened to his words.

"You are God's sons and daughters, and you have the freedom to be yourself," he said.

During his talk, the word *freedom* hit me hard. To think that I was free. The air seemed clearer, the sky bluer, the flowers much prettier and more fragrant than ever before. Was that what Jesus meant when he spoke of freedom and being a child of the heavenly Father? The way he spoke of the Father was so different from our concept of gods like Jupiter, the god of the heavens and the grape harvest. Suddenly I saw a butterfly move past me, gaily flying from one flower to another, bright and free. I often thought, while Jesus spoke, that men and women were meant to be as free and as beautiful as the butterfly. We were not meant to crawl in the dirt as a caterpillar does.

It's funny how much more meaning the word *freedom* has for me now. Jesus went on talking of the Father's love for each of us, His desire for our happiness. I felt so clean, so free of guilt, as if my past had finally been washed away. At that thought, Jesus glanced my way. His look told me that he understood. I smiled, my heart full of joy. He nodded his approval and continued his teaching.

～ *Paula* ～

How magnificent he looked in his white robe, with the deep blue sky as a backdrop! I listened to his words while resting against a huge rock, surrounded by blades of grass and gentle sprouts of daffodils. He spoke with such authority about the love of his Father—a love and concern we should all have for each other. He spoke also of the need for prayer, and a positive attitude. Such a silent hush engulfed the crowd when he uttered those seemingly magic words:

"Happy are you when your interest is focused on God, for no matter what anyone does to you, you will not fear, retaliate, or seek vengeance. You will not pursue jealous endeavors and create bitter campaigns against the persecutors.

"No, you shall remain at peace, calm and tranquil, trusting your God. Your enemy will not be allowed to get the upper hand, because he will be fighting against God, who is Love. You must be compassionate, understanding, and kind—seeking union, not division.

"Prayer must be at one with your beliefs. When you pray, pray from the heart. Talk to your Divine Parent as you would a friend, a beloved, one who means more to you than the world. Speak in honesty and sincerity, without masks or pretense. Call Him Daddy, for He is just that, wishing to call you to Him and embrace you with all of the love His heart will hold. Call him Lover if you wish, for His love is so great that your heart overflows in His presence.

"Also, call your Parent the Divine Nurturer, for She gives us all we need in order to find life a celebration. Call Her Merciful One, for She forgives us our human faults, our countless sins, and teaches us to forgive ourselves and others. Call Her Protector, for She preserves us from darkness, and Her words become our light, our life, our path, leading us on to glory and triumph, toward a new dawn."

Oh, how my heart leapt in my chest upon learning Jesus' words of comfort. No more would I falter and fumble. He has become my light. He has become my life, this man called Jesus.

Nicodemus, a Teacher

I have been teaching the law so long that I had forgotten the essentials of life. This Jesus has started a revolution without weapons; armed only with love, he creates a new world. I must talk to him, but I can't allow my fellow teachers to see me or I would become an outcast to my profession, my religion, my country. They are upset because he speaks of love, elevating this virtue higher than the law. If only I had the courage to let myself go entirely, to make his way my way. But I am not yet ready for total surrender. I might lose my job! O Lord in heaven, give me a sign, some kind of miracle, something extravagant.

Just knowing Jesus has made me a happier person than I was when I pursued the smallest iota of the law. Could that be my sign? Hasn't someone said that our greatest miracle is the change we make in our own life? If only I could be sure. I will spend more time with Jesus. He doesn't mind that I come in the darkness of night when the only noise heard is the hoot of the owls and the screeching of crickets. Jesus probably wonders about my lack of courage, but he would never be so unkind as to mention it. Well, he's not alone. I'm beginning to wonder about it myself.

Parmenos, Another Teacher
of Religion

Jesus was in a discussion with a few of my fellow Pharisees one day when I realized that he had some very good ideas on religion. My brethren grew angry with him because of his teachings, however, and left. I stayed behind so I might ask him a few questions. "Master," I said, "what is the most important of all the commandments?"

I can remember the gleam in his eyes when he answered, "You must love the Lord your God with your whole being, and love your neighbor in the same way as you love yourself. No other commandments are greater than these."

His answer burned into my heart because it was so practical, so honest. Love others, but first learn to love yourself. That's really what he meant: to love God so much that you let God's Spirit operate from within you. His approach is so logical and so natural that it is unique. We Pharisees are so wrapped up in law that we cannot see the real truths in life. When Jesus speaks of love, he fills us with an unusual sense of joy, as if there were no end to the beauty of springtime. For his love is, in a sense, the springtime of the soul, the springtime of the spirit, the springtime of God within! It is not an abstraction, an empty word, but life at its core. Maybe this is why my fellow teachers are so angry with Jesus. He gives meaning and substance to living and to loving. He's a man of beauty, a man of depth, and, most of all, a true man of God.

Bartholomew,
an Apostle

Jesus was a very clever man when it came to his enemies, the Pharisees, who were always attempting to trap him. They hated him because he was so popular, and in public they would gather like vultures waiting to ask trivial questions regarding the law. I recall one such incident on the Sabbath when some of us were walking through a field. Somewhat hungry, we broke off the heads of wheat, rubbed the husks together in our hands, and ate the grains.

A group of Pharisees standing nearby shouted out, "That's illegal and immoral!" One would think that was all they knew how to say. Then they said that working on the Sabbath was against Jewish law and God's law. No one asked if we were hungry, but Jesus retorted almost immediately.

"King David took special bread offered to the Lord when his men were hungry, and they ate it," he said. "That was illegal, too."

The Pharisees stood there dumbfounded. They weren't able to answer Jesus without talking against King David, which a good Jew would never do. Those Pharisees were so legal-minded that they became unreasonable and impractical. If a mule fell into a water hole on the Sabbath, they would let it drown rather than save it, because saving it would entail work. That kind of attitude is impractical and pointless. Jesus was more concerned with being practical. He wanted us to use our brains, our talents, and our common sense. Those are all gifts from the heavenly Father so that we can be happy. Jesus never asked us to abandon our God-given rights. I loved him—not so much because of his high degree of intelligence, but rather for his earthy approach to life. It was refreshing.

The

HEALING POWER

of

SILENCE

and

SOLITUDE

～ A Man of the Desert ～

Jesus of Nazareth—a name I will never forget. He came into the desert seeking solitude for 40 days of prayer. As he journeyed to an isolated spot, we encountered each other and talked about the presence of the Almighty and the need to be alone, to become one with the universe, creation, all living things, and God Himself.

At first I thought him to be a confused man, but soon I realized that he was a great human being. I watched him as he strolled along the rocky cliffs, stopping occasionally to pick up grains of sand and small pebbles, perhaps to study their composition and nature. He would smile and gently replace them as if not wishing to hurt them. He was a man to admire. At night when the air was still and the moon shone over the desert like a great pearl hanging aloft in a dark, endless sky, we sat and prayed together. I felt lifted from this earth, as if my body were weightless.

God's presence engulfed and embraced my very being. Once again, I fell in love with my God. You see, although I lived in the desert, my love had grown cold and my God had gone far away. I had lost sight of heaven and earth, and in so doing had created a living hell for myself. The desert can be a place of death and anguish or a place of life and beauty. It is our attitude and closeness to God that determines whether where we live is heaven or hell. Just by my being within his presence, Jesus gave me new insight, new life, a world filled with heaven.

The desert is still a home for me although Jesus is no longer here in body. But somehow, out here in the evening stillness, in the brilliant sunsets and peaceful quietude, I know he listens and hears me, for a friend is never far away, even in the desert.

The
HEALING POWER
of the
SPOKEN WORD

Artemus, a Poet Living
~ in Galilee ~

Whenever he spoke, Jesus' words pulsated with the rhythm of enthusiasm and life. No ordinary man, Jesus was a divine poet uniting earthbound humanity with all that is heavenly. Sometimes he spoke words we didn't understand because we were not ready to meet the joys of life head-on. Often we misunderstood this poet because we misunderstood life itself. We were confused by his joy, for we had none of our own.

Jesus had a way with words that informed the lifeless, gave new birth to the dying spirit, provoked the hypocrites, and brought peace of mind to the living. The valleys and meadows rang with the sound of heaven as he spoke to his multitude of followers. Even the flowers and every blade of grass seemed to be listening as they swayed gently back and forth in the early springtime breeze, keeping rhythm with every word flowing from the mouth of this divine poet. His whole existence was a prayer embracing all living things. He was indeed the Way, the Truth, the Life, a light put to death by those who hate the truth and prefer the dread, bitter hell of darkness.

Christianus,
⬛ *a Follower of Jesus* ⬛

T he day I first heard him teach, I wasn't sure if I liked him or not. But his words grew on me. Soon I found myself following him from town to town, listening intently as he taught people the bright side of life. He taught them how to see the sun even when it was not shining. Yes, he would tell them it was still there, even if we didn't see it. Jesus would tell us to seek happiness always, under all circumstances. "Happy are you even if you mourn, for you shall be comforted. Happy are you when you practice kindness and mercy. Happy are the sincere." His words rang through me like so many bells shattering the stillness of the night air. "When people talk about you because you are my followers, be happy; don't let it disturb your peace of mind. Your reward will be great."

Often his words would pierce my heart and give me new insight: "I have come that you may live abundantly." How true, Jesus. I have lived now like I have never lived before. The past was mere existence. The present and future are life.

CELEBRATING
GRATITUDE

~ *The Samaritan Woman* ~

How hot and dry it was that summer day when I went to the well to draw upon God's natural resource—cool, sparkling water to quench my thirst. That's what I needed so badly, at least I thought so.

There was this man, the Nazarene, sitting by the well. He smiled at me with a gentle, loving smile unlike any I've ever seen. The man told me that what I really needed was living water. *Living water,* I thought. *What an unusual thing to say.* Then he began to speak to me in a way no one had ever spoken, telling me that he could give me these living waters. I listened, my heart filled to overflowing with joy. I realized what Jesus meant by living waters—his words, his life, and his spirit were all as refreshing as the pure waters that bubbled up from the undergound springs around our village. All at once I felt alive, reborn with this water of which Jesus spoke.

Always to drink of this water is still my strongest desire, to be filled with the water of this living, eternal fountain of youth. For what is eternal youth but everlasting joy, love, and undying enthusiasm for life itself?

Silas, a Man Back
⸺ from Fishing with His Son ⸺

On the way back from fishing in the Sea of Galilee, my son and I observed a crowd gathering around some man whom I had never before seen. "Who is that?" I asked someone.

"It's Jesus of Nazareth," they replied. I had heard many people speak his name, but I had never met him. My son and I sat down near Jesus so we could hear him more easily. At this point, some of his followers were arguing frantically among themselves. They were talking about how the crowd was hungry but there was no food. I had to agree with the one disciple who said that people would not listen to God's word on an empty stomach.

Jesus overhead them talking and asked them to find some food. Now my son and I had managed to catch a few small fish, but certainly not enough to begin to feed such a multitude as this. Then Jesus' eyes met mine, and he glanced at the fish lying in my basket. I looked at him, startled, but somehow I knew he wanted those fish. I told my son to take them to Jesus. With a smile on his face, Jesus placed his hand on my son's head and kindly said, "Thank you, young man. You are a good boy."

My boy jumped for joy at this act of kindness, since most grown men do not treat children who are not their own with affection. Sometimes I, too, forget how much love means to children. They want to be taken into our arms and be told they are loved and very much appreciated. Jesus even winked at me, telling me in a way that he knew what I was thinking. Jesus then bowed his head and prayed. We did the same.

Shortly afterwards, he began passing out my fish. The supply seemed endless. It was a miracle! From a few fishes and loaves of bread that someone else had donated, Jesus provided plenty. It was an event my son and I talked about for weeks and even months. And you know, my little boy has never forgotten that one, solitary act of kindness—and neither have I.

~ Zaccheus ~

Here comes the crowd, and Jesus is in the center. I've got to see him. But how? Where can I go? I've got to catch a glimpse of him before he passes me by. I know, I'll climb this sycamore tree. It will be a little rough because I'm not as good at this as I once was, but for Jesus I'll do it. Here he comes. I'm so excited. I see him! I see him! The Son of Man.

How gentle he looks, how kind and considerate! If I tell him my problems and troubles, he's sure to listen. No one else will talk to me, because they hate me. Once upon a time, I stole from people, but I've confessed my faults and changed my ways. I won't do it again. Please, someone, forgive me. Be my friend.

Oh, Jesus, please hear me. He's stopping. He's looking up here and motioning for me to come forward. I'm coming, Jesus. Please don't leave. I'm coming. Oh, Jesus, forgive me. I've been wrong. Say you'll be my friend. Your eyes are so compassionate, so understanding. I know you believe me. Oh, thank you, Jesus. Oh, thank you. You've changed my life. I can sing and dance again. Thank you, Jesus. Thank you!

~ A Child ~

I remember when I first saw him in the grassy meadows near the sea. It was a hot, sunny afternoon, the birds flying overhead, the sky a peaceful blue, everything tranquil. He motioned for me to come over to him. He seemed friendly, his eyes full of compassion, his voice soft and understanding. He showed none of the bitterness and hectoring dogma of so many of the other preachers of our day. No, he was calm, almost serene, full of faith and love. He put his arm on my shoulder that day like no one has done for years. They all think that once you've reached the age of 13, you don't need affection anymore. How far from the truth they are! We need it, believe me, now more than ever.

He spoke to me as a gentle father would, explaining the truths of life, the necessity of love, the beauty of friendship. My heart swelled with love for this man, so much more love than I ever knew in all my life. Why couldn't others take time out for me as Jesus did? I'm not a bad boy. He was what I've been searching for—someone to turn to, someone to care for me who wouldn't fear showing me affection. He was someone I could love and who would love me, a father figure in the true sense of that phrase.

"I never want to leave your side, Jesus," I said. He smiled knowingly, and the peaceful tones of his voice rippled gently from his mouth as the water ripples softly across the lake when touched by a summer breeze. "You will never have to leave me, John."

Zebedee, a Sailor

I was sitting on the dock near the seashore getting my boat ready for the next catch when he walked nearby, his hair flowing in the breeze. He waved and asked if I were a sailor. "Yes," I said.

"A noble profession," he replied. "Being near God's creation, working with your hands."

That was my first glimpse of Jesus, the man everyone was talking about. He acted like any other man, except that he seemed a lot happier. He would brush back his long, flowing hair as he talked. His brown eyes, set deep within his olive-colored face, sparkled and danced so gaily. Often he would remove his outer garments and dive into the water near the dock. "Swimming is so refreshing," he would say as he splashed about.

The fish would encircle him in the water, having no fear, and in fact seeming to play around him. *Unusual,* I thought. As Jesus seemed to talk and whisper to them, they would dash to and fro as if playing a game of hide and seek. Oh, that man was unique and playful. He would tell me how much God loved me for taking care of his creation, the seas, while working so hard to feed others the food God provides for his children. Then he would dry his hair and body in the warm summer sun, put on his undergarments and tunic, then whisper,

"Farewell until we meet again, my friend. Take care of the seas, for I shall be back this way again to swim."

Farewell for now, and take care, my friend.

Inspirational
Reading

Borg, Marcus, ed. *Jesus and Buddha: The Parallel Sayings.* Berkeley, Cal.: Seastone, 1997.

Davis, Avram. *The Way of Flame: A Guide to the Forgotten Mystical Tradition of Jewish Meditation.* San Francisco: HarperSanFrancisco, 1996.

Franciscan Friars of the Immaculate Conception. *Padre Pio: The Wonder Worker.* Waite Park, Minn.: Park Press, Inc., 1999.

Nouwen, Henri J. M. *The Only Necessary Thing: Living a Prayerful Life.* Compiled and edited by Wendy Wilson Greer. New York: Crossroad, 1999.

——. *Making All Things New: An Invitation to the Spiritual Life.* San Francisco: HarperSanFrancisco, 1981.

——. *Here and Now: Living in the Spirit.* New York: Crossroad, 1995.

——. *Life of the Beloved: Spiritual Living in a Secular World.* New York: Crossroad, 1992.

Roth, Ron, with Peter Occhiogrosso. *The Healing Path of Prayer: The Modern Mystic's Guide to Spiritual Power*. New York: Three Rivers, 1997.

———. *Prayer and the Five Stages of Healing*. Carlsbad, Cal.: Hay House, 1998.

Schmidt, Joseph F. *Praying with Thérèse of Lisieux*. Winona, Minn.: Saint Mary's Press, 1992.

The Secret Teachings of Jesus: Four Gnostic Gospels. Translated by Marvin W. Meyer. New York: Random House, 1984.

Stoutzenberger, Joseph M. and John D. Bohrer. *Praying with Francis of Assisi*. Winona, Minn., Saint Mary's Press, 1989.

Ward, Benedicta, S.L.G. *The Desert Christian: Sayings of the Desert Fathers*. New York: Macmillan, 1975.

The Way of a Pilgrim and The Pilgrim Continues His Way. Trans. by R.M. French. San Francisco: HarperSanFrancisco, 1991.

World Scripture: A Comparative Anthology of Sacred Texts. Edited by Andrew Wilson. New York: Paragon House, 1995.

Yogananda, Paramahansa. *In the Sancturary of the Soul: A Guide to Effective Prayer*. Los Angeles: Self-Realization Fellowship, 1998.

Please note: A new sacred oil that has been developed for Ron Roth will be available through the Celebrating Life Institute. For information, consult his Website at: **www.ronroth.com.**

About
the Author

Ron Roth, Ph.D., is an internationally known teacher, spiritual healer, and modern-day mystic. As a leading-edge voice bringing us into the New Millennium, he has appeared on many television and radio programs, including *The Oprah Winfrey Show.* Ron is the author of several books, including the bestseller *The Healing Path of Prayer* and the audiocassette *Healing Prayers.* He served in the Roman Catholic priesthood for more than 25 years and is the founder of the Celebrating Life Institute in Peru, Illinois, where he lives. You can contact Ron Roth at: **www.ronroth.com.**

Other Hay House Titles
of Related Interest

Books

The Experience of God, edited by Jonathan Robinson

Experiencing the Soul, by Eliot Jay Rosen

God, Creation, and Tools for Life, by Sylvia Browne

Handle with Prayer, by Alan Cohen

The Jesus Code, by John Randolph Price

7 Paths to God, by Joan Borysenko, Ph.D.

Audios

All about God, a Dialogue Between Neale Donald
Walsch and Deepak Chopra, M.D.

Healing with the Angels, by Doreen Virtue, Ph.D.

Pathways to God, a Dialogue Between Joan
Borysenko, Ph.D., and Deepak Chopra, M.D.

We hope you enjoyed this Hay House book.
If you would like to receive a free catalog
featuring additional Hay House books and products,
or if you would like information about the
Hay Foundation, please contact:

Hay House, Inc.
P.O. Box 5100
Carlsbad, CA 92018-5100

(760) 431-7695 or **(800) 654-5126**
(760) 431-6948 (fax) or **(800) 650-5115 (fax)**

Please visit the Hay House Website at:
www.hayhouse.com